TRIANGLES
OF FIRE

TORKOM
SARAYDARIAN

SARAYDARIAN
INSTITUTE
P. O. BOX 267 · SEDONA, AZ 86339

Library of Congress Number: 77-82155
ISBN: 0-911794-35-2

Cover Design: Fine Point Graphics
                     Sedona, Arizona

Typography: C. S. Epstein

Printed by Delta Lithograph Co., Valencia, California

Printed in the United States of America

NOTE: The exercises and meditations given in this book
should be used only after receiving professional advice. Use
them with greatest discretion thereafter, and at your own
risk.

Dedicated to
Foster Bailey
and
Mary Bailey.

About
the Author

*T*orkom Saraydarian was born in Asia Minor. Since childhood he has tried to understand the mystery called man.

He visited monasteries, ancient temples and mystery schools in order to find the answers to his burning questions.

He lived with Sufis, dervishes, Christian mystics and masters of temple music and dance. It took long years of discipline and sacrifice to absorb the Ageless Wisdom from its true sources. Meditation became a part of his daily life and service a natural expression of his soul.

Torkom Saraydarian is the author of thirty books, which are read throughout the world. They have been translated into German, Dutch, Danish, Portuguese, French, Spanish, Italian and Greek. He has lectured in many cities; he has written numerous articles in philosophical and religious publications.

He is a violinist, pianist, composer, teacher, lecturer, mechanical engineer, meteorologist, writer and philosopher.

Contents

The Great Invocation

From the point of Light within the
      Mind of God
Let light stream forth into the
      minds of men.
Let Light descend on Earth.

From the point of Love within the
      Heart of God
Let love stream forth into the
      hearts of men.
May Christ return to Earth.

From the centre where the
      Will of God is known
Let purpose guide the little
      wills of men—
The purpose which the Masters
      know and serve.

From the centre which we call the
      race of men
Let the Plan of Love and Light
      work out
And may it seal the door where
      evil dwells.

Let Light and Love and Power
      restore the Plan on Earth.

Keyword

[T]he triangle is the basic geometric form of all manifestation and it is to be seen . . . underlying the entire fabric of manifestation, whether it is the manifestation of a solar system, the manifestation of the zodiacal round, the cosmic triplicities or the tiny reflection of this divine triple whole which we call man.[1]

—Master Djwhal Khul—

---

[1]Bailey, Alice A., *Esoteric Astrology*, p. 429.

1

The Teaching
Concerning
Triangles

*I*n 1945, a great sage, Master Djwhal Khul, gave humanity the esoteric teaching on triangles. This teaching is found throughout all His writings, particularly in:

> *Esoteric Astrology*
> *The Reappearance of the Christ*
> *Discipleship in the New Age*, Vols. I and II
> *The Rays and the Initiations*
> *The Externalisation of the Hierarchy*
> *Esoteric Psychology*, Vols. I and II

All of these books are published by the Lucis Publishing Company, New York, a non-profit organization owned by the Lucis Trust. The Lucis Trust also has two centers in Europe — one in London and one in Geneva — thus forming a triangle of light within these three great planetary centers, through which the Teaching of the New Age is distributed to humanity.

In the past forty years, the teaching of triangles has penetrated into almost all countries of the world and has generated millions of triangles.

A triangle is composed of three people who say the *Great Invocation* daily to invoke light, love and power, in order to create peace, understanding, cooperation, abundance and freedom.

There are triangles that invoke light; there are triangles that spread goodwill; and there are triangles that are in preparation to serve as circulatory agents for will energy.

How to Form a Triangle of Light.

This is a very easy process. First, find two friends. Give them a copy of the *Great Invocation*, and explain to them how it is a world prayer, a world invocation which will open the human mind to incoming light, open the human heart to incoming love, and blend human will with Divine Will, thus preparing the way for the reappearance of Christ, helping humanity to walk the path of righteousness, beauty, simplicity, gratitude and joy.

Once they accept and love the *Great Invocation* and practice sounding it, ask them if they would like to say it at the same time every day, visualizing each other as points of light, love and power through which Divine Light, Divine Love and Divine Power can circulate and radiate out to the field of all of their human relationships.

If they agree, set an appropriate time for all three of you, and begin saying the *Great Invocation* at the appointed time every day. It is possible that some participants may occasionally be late, or they may forget to sound it for certain reasons. Never mind; just continue doing it, periodically communicating with each other and sharing your experiences and joys.

Sometimes if one person forgets to say the *Great Invocation*, he will telepathically awaken and remember when the others start. It is enough if one of the participants is awake; eventually he will be able to call the others to their sacred duty.

After the first triangle is firmly established, you can start other triangles to be repeated at different times, proceeding in the same way. If any participant cannot continue in his task for any reason, then he must be kind enough to inform the other two so that they can choose another person for their triangle.

It is advisable not to have more than five triangles, because **the most important ingredients in a triangle are enthusiasm, livingness, joy and vitality.** It should not be turned into a mechanical action, but should be a task to which each participant looks forward.

You must remember that the power of the Invocation increases as you put real interest, attention, pure visualization and creative thinking into it. This means that your mind must concentrate upon the words you are saying. The words must be said slowly, with solemnity, and you must not waver over your problems, worries or plans as you repeat it. At the time you say the *Great Invocation*, you must raise your consciousness as high as possible, detaching your mind from personal problems and interests, focusing it on those great concepts and visions found in the *Great Invocation*.

In repeating the *Great Invocation*:

1. First, visualize the other two triangle participants sitting in the room with you, sitting together in Nature, or in any pleasant setting.

2. Then visualize a golden thread linking all three of you, thus forming a living, fiery triangle.

3. Then focus your mind as high as possible, and solemnly begin to repeat the *Great Invocation*.

4. Between stanzas, pause and visualize the triangle participants anew, before going on to the next stanza.

5. After you have completed the *Great Invocation*, sit relaxed for a moment, and then silently go about your work.

You must remember that all of this must be performed in a totally relaxed and joyful way. No stress or strain must be attached to this sacred work. Any time you feel that you are tense, nervous or exhausted, rest, find yourself and relax before saying the *Great Invocation*, even if you are an hour late.

You can sit cross-legged if you wish; you can sit on a chair, or if outside, on a rock. Wherever you sit, try to hold your spine erect and relaxed. Do not mix any other meditation practices with this task. Give special attention to it, and really make it special. You can even light a candle, burn a stick of sandalwood incense, and dress in a special, beautiful, clean robe before saying the *Great Invocation*.

All of these practices are helpful, but they are not necessary if you are ready to concentrate, focus fully and uplift yourself to a higher state of consciousness. In this sense, concentration is an intense focus of mental energy, charged with the purpose of this great mantram, carried to the Soul, or to Hierarchical spheres, demanding an answer, which is called **evocation**.

This means that, as much as possible, the person should concentrate his mind on the meaning of the *Great Invocation*, fixing his mind on the "door" upon which he will knock by sounding it. He should not allow any random thoughts to enter his mental sphere which interfere with his concentration.

It sometimes happens that unexpected guests will arrive at the time you are preparing to say the Invocation. You can still do it. Invite them in and tell them that you will be with them in a few minutes. Then go to your private room, close the door, and detach yourself as much as possible. Forget your guests, and enter the sanctuary of your Soul. Communicate with the centers of Light, Love and Power. Then after a minute of silence, return to your guests. It is very likely that they will notice a new beauty in your face and mannerisms, and greater wisdom in your words.

If you are driving along the highway at the appointed time, pull your car to the side and park for a few minutes while you attend to your triangle work. You will drive with greater joy and relaxation thereafter.

Triangle work becomes more potent and its effect more far-reaching, when we consider for a moment the psychological tools with which every triangle participant can work on his own level of achievement.

1. Memorize the *Great Invocation* and at certain times of the day, ponder the meaning of certain phrases and words. Deepen your penetration into the meaning and significance of the words.

2. When it is time to contact the other two triangle participants, sit quietly and lift your con-

sciousness as high as possible, detaching your-self from all physical, emotional and mental concerns.

3. Visualize the points of the triangle, the two other people who are ready to sound the *Great Invocation* with you.

   A. See a beam of light projecting from the middle point of your forehead, reaching the first person.

   B. Then see another beam of light reaching the second person. Make your visualization as clear as possible, without strain or stress.

   C. See the beam of light uniting all three triangle participants.

   D. Visualize the energies of Light, Love and Power circulating through the beam of light.

   E. Visualize Christ, shining as pure light in the center of the triangle.

4. Start to sound the *Great Invocation* word for word, with great concentration. At the same time, invoke the energies of Light, Love and Power into the center of the triangle, spreading through that center along the beam of light forming the triangle and circulating through the three points of the triangle. Thus, the points of the triangle set into motion three Divine Energies in a triangular formation, filling the triangular space with the energies of Divine Light, Love and Power. When these energies continue to flow in a triangular for-

mation, they transect square etheric patterns and change them into triangular patterns.

Alignment is very important in dealing with states of consciousness and with energies and forces coming from great centers in the planet and Universe. Alignment is a process of connecting communication lines with the power house, or station, to channel energies, impressions and inspiration without distortion or dissipation.

In this case, the line of communication is our consciousness thread, which is anchored in the brain, extending itself slowly through the etheric brain to the mental body, anchoring itself in the Soul or at the center of the twelve-petaled Lotus in the head. This thread bypasses the astral body, linking the brain with the head center and the twelve-petaled Lotus in the higher mind.

When this alignment is established, the *Great Invocation* is then sounded on Soul levels, or in the abstract mind, with such power that it creates an evocation from the Hierarchy and from great centers of Light in the Universe. The full power of the *Great Invocation* is demonstrated only when one sounds it on Soul levels.

We are told that all mantrams are on the Second Ray of Love-Wisdom, and that the Soul is primarily a source or channel for such love. Such an alignment not only conditions the undisturbed flow of energy from Higher Sources, but it also provides protection from dark forces, which seek any opportunity to interfere with such work.

The astral plane is the plane of glamor; it is from this plane that the dark forces operate, possess and control people. It is on this plane that glamors are contacted and even absorbed into our system. It is from this plane that dark forces descend on Earth to prevent progress, as best as they can.

That is why in the process of alignment, we must bypass this plane, and through our visualization build a golden line of communication between the Soul and the brain. This will prevent the dark forces from making any contact with our triangle work. Such an alignment will slowly develop, helping us to contact the Hierarchy, particularly Christ, bringing in a flow of great inspiration for creative work and for the welfare of humanity.

Alignment eventually builds a cross-like symbol. Vertically, man will contact his Soul, his Master, the Hierarchy, the Christ. Horizontally, he will contact all those triangles in the world that work for the transformation of the planet. This is how the network of light, goodwill, and will-to-good is built.

A disciple or Initiate is one who works with energies. He learns how to invoke, how to direct, how to precipitate, and how to use energies for the service of humanity. His greatest tools are **visualization, creative imagination and directed projection**. Through visualization we contact future patterns, the prototypes; through creative imagination we vest them with proper forms and mechanisms; through projection we set them into motion and put them to use.

Those who continue their triangle work year after year will eventually discover that they are becoming skilled in using mental substance. Unless a person is able to use his mind creatively, he cannot help the evolution of humanity; he cannot manipulate and direct energy; he cannot be a bridge by which others may achieve; he cannot cause the flow of energy to move from subjective centers to the field of objective activity.

5. The next step is to radiate out the accumulated energy within the triangle to the entire world. By using creative imagination, one can "see" the energy of Light, Love and Power flowing into the whole network of triangles in the etheric body of humanity, increasing in that network the energies of Light and Love, and sensitivity to Divine Purpose and Divine Will, leading this planet "from darkness to light, from chaos to beauty."

6. After completing this step, sit very quietly for a few moments. Recollect where you are sitting; feel your body. This completes your triangle task. It is beneficial to remain silent for at least a few minutes afterwards.

7. During the day, register any ideas that occur to your mind regarding the triangle work. Share them with the other "points," if you think that your recordings will deepen their knowledge and create greater interest in them toward the triangle work.

8. It is very important to often consider the *Great Invocation*, pondering it from various angles.

You grow by thinking. Thinking is the result of contact, and a reaction to contact. You contact the energy hidden within a word, a sentence, or within the whole Invocation. After this contact, you build your own form of interpretation, your own symbol of explanation. Through this building process, you translate the unknown into knowledge.

The whole solar system is the result of contact that the Greater Life makes with greater vision, greater purpose beyond Himself. As He tries to understand, His creation comes into being. His creation — this solar system — is the manifestation of His thought. Our creativity is the direct result of our understanding of the unknown. There is no creation or creativity without thinking.

Formless meditation is a kind of meditation through which one creates forms from intuitional substances, or from light substance, which cannot be observed on the level of matter. Due to their subtlety, electrical forms cannot be registered by the brain, because of the present level of development of our mechanism.

It is possible to think on formless levels and not register any specific symbols on the mental plane. This is what *Samadhi* is. Because the Initiate is active on the Intuitional Plane, he does not need to register it on the lower plane, unless it is necessary for certain service. It is noted that such higher level contacts often express themselves as radioactive healing energy, magnetism, perfume, or some other kind of energy which expands your consciousness, causes striving within you, challenges you toward purity and beauty, and annihilates many prison walls from around you.

Thinking helps you in the process of illumination. Once you are enlightened, it manifests itself in many ways, building many forms on various planes. This is how form comes into being.

There are states of awareness which seem thoughtless to us. But if a person in that condition contacts his students or friends, he tries to think, to explain what the thoughtless state is. Let us remember that we are living in the Cosmic Physical Plane, which means that it is impossible for us to reach a formless state of awareness or consciousness, even on the highest plane, the Divine Plane.

Those who enter into higher planes of the Cosmic Physical Plane become invisible to the lower planes, but they still create subtle forms as they come into contact with both higher and lower levels of reality.

In triangle work, we must use our creativity to build those forms which will express or radiate greater energy to the entire field of human evolution. This starts with deep thinking and by contacting the energies of the *Great Invocation*.

2

The Esoteric Idea Behind Triangles

*J*ust as every living form has an energy field around itself, our planet also has its electromagnetic sphere of energy. This energy penetrates all parts of the planet, penetrates all forms, and at the same time extends out into Space as a field of energy within which our planet lives, moves and has its being.

Not only this planet, but also the entire solar system has its energy field. It is this energy field which ties all forms together into one life. Master Djwhal Khul, in speaking on this subject, says:

> [T]he ether of space is the field in and through which the energies from the many originating Sources play. We are, therefore, concerned with the etheric body of the planet, of the solar system, and of the seven solar systems of which our system is one, as well as with the general and vaster etheric body of the universe in which we are located. I employ the word "located" here with deliberation and because of the inferences to which it leads. This vaster field, as well as the smaller and more localised fields, provide the

medium of transmission for all the energies which play upon and through our solar system, our planetary spheres and all forms of life upon those spheres. It forms one unbroken field of activity in constant ceaseless motion — an eternal medium for the exchange and transmission of energies.

In connection with this . . . [e]sotericism teaches . . . that underlying the physical body and its comprehensive and intricate system of nerves is a vital or etheric body which is the counterpart and the true form of the outer and tangible phenomenal aspect. It is likewise the medium for the transmission of force to all parts of the human frame and the agent of the indwelling life and consciousness. It determines and conditions the physical body, for it is itself the repository and the transmitter of energy from the various subjective aspects of man and also from the environment in which man (both inner and outer man) finds himself.

Two other points should here be added. First: the individual etheric body is not an isolated and separated human vehicle, but is, in a peculiar sense, an integral part of the etheric body of that entity which we have called the human family; this kingdom in nature, through its etheric body, is an integral part of the planetary etheric body; the planetary etheric body is not separated off from the etheric bodies of other planets but all of them in their totality, along with the etheric body of the sun constitute the etheric body of the solar system. This is related to the etheric bodies of the six solar systems which, with ours, form a cosmic unity and into these pour energies and forces from certain great constellations. The field of space is etheric in nature and its vital body is composed of the totality of etheric bodies of all constellations, solar systems and planets which are found therein. Throughout this cosmic golden web there is a constant circulation of energies and forces and this constitutes the scientific basis of the astrological theories.[1]

All of these solar systems, planets and individuals have energy vortexes in their etheric bodies, which act as centers of reception, assimilation and distribution.

We are told that the pattern of the circulation of energy in the etheric body of the planet is square. Four centers are connected with each other in the circulation of force. Such a pattern creates concretion, materialization, and builds the "foundation." But if such a pattern lasts longer than required for its purpose, it creates degeneration and deterioration in the forms.

Our etheric bodies and the etheric body of the planet are built from threads of force through which the energy of life circulates. For example, we are told that the pattern of circulation of energy for non-sacred planets is the pattern of the square; that of sacred planets is triangular in formation; and that of the sun is circular.

---

[1]Bailey, Alice A., *Esoteric Astrology*, pp. 9-11.

The same rule applies to human beings. An average person's aura shows square circulation. But if he becomes a Third Degree Initiate, a transfigured person, the whole pattern of energy circulation is triangular; and if he becomes a Master, the triangular circulation becomes circular.

We must mention here that all squares, triangles and circles are not of the same magnitude. They have their own evolution in which they gradually grow brighter and brighter, until they become very fiery. After reaching a stage of extremely intense radioactivity, squares become triangles, and triangles change into circles.

In the case of triangles, a dim outline of the triangle appears at first. It gets brighter and more vibrant, and eventually, at the center of the triangle, a fiery nucleus appears around which the triangle begins to revolve at progressively higher speeds.

The form, intensity of light, and the rate of revolution determine the quantity, quality and voltage of energy passing through the points, thus affecting the dense physical body, the emotional and mental systems, and radiating out to the environment, causing fundamental changes in the structure of the human life.

Master Djwhal Khul, in speaking about triangles, tabulates the various triangles on various levels, as follows:

1. *The pranic triangle.*
   a. The shoulder centre.
   b. The centre near the diaphragm.
   c. The spleen.

2. *Man controlled from the astral plane.*
   a. The base of the spine.

  b. The solar plexus.
  c. The heart.

3. *Man controlled from the mental plane.*
  a. The base of the spine.
  b. The heart.
  c. The throat.

4. *Man partially controlled by the Ego, advanced man.*
  a. The heart.
  b. The throat.
  c. The head, i.e., the four lesser centres and their synthesis, the alta centre.

5. *Spiritual man to the third Initiation.*
  a. The heart.
  b. The throat.
  c. The seven head centres.

6. *Spiritual man to the fifth Initiation.*
  a. The heart.
  b. The seven head centres.
  c. The two many-petalled lotuses.[2]

These triangles have their correspondences in the planet, in the solar system, and in the Cosmos. For example, there are Humanity, the Hierarchy and Shamballa. There are:

  Venus, Uranus, Earth;
  Saturn, Uranus, Mercury.

There are:

  Pleiades, Cancer, Venus;
  Great Bear, Aries, Pluto;

---

[2]Bailey, Alice A., *A Treatise on Cosmic Fire*, pp. 169-170.

> Sirius, Leo, Jupiter;
> Leo, Saturn, Shamballa;
> Pisces, Uranus, the Hierarchy;
> Capricorn, Mercury, Humanity;
> Sirius, Pleiades, Great Bear;
> Leo, Pisces, Capricorn.

All of these greater or lesser centers link together in triangular formation for certain tasks within the network of the energy in Space.

Master Djwhal Khul says that at the present time Leo—Pisces—Capricorn, and Saturn—Uranus—Mercury are vitalizing and stimulating three planetary centers: Shamballa, the Hierarchy and Humanity.

> Behind these three stands a cosmic triangle, emanating three streams of energy which pour into and through the three lesser triangles, thus potently affecting every kingdom in nature. This cosmic triangle is that of the *Great Bear — Sirius — the Pleiades*.[3]

In *Esoteric Astrology*, Master Djwhal Khul lists many triangles of energy within the Zodiac. We can channel greater energy by forming our triangles according to our astrological signs, using our sun sign or rising sign. For example, if you are a Scorpio, you can choose your triangle members from those whose signs are Taurus, Sagittarius, Gemini, Virgo and Capricorn. It seems to me that in this way we give additional power to our triangle work by attracting the energies of these constellations, using them in the work of building a new web for the planetary body.

---

[3]Bailey, Alice A., *Esoteric Astrology*, p. 441.

These are the suggested triangles:

Aries, Leo, Capricorn
Gemini, Virgo, Pisces
Cancer, Libra, Capricorn
Taurus, Scorpio, Sagittarius
Leo, Sagittarius, Aquarius
Virgo, Sagittarius, Pisces
Aries, Cancer, Capricorn
Leo, Virgo, Pisces
Gemini, Scorpio, Virgo
Capricorn, Leo, Virgo
Leo, Libra, Sagittarius
Taurus, Scorpio, Capricorn
Taurus, Pisces, Aquarius

It is interesting to note that square patterns and triangular formations also appear in our horoscopes. Esoterically, they are very significant. Those who have triangular formations are mostly disciples and Initiates. Those who have squares are average, or are people who are not yet in harmony with their Soul or Spiritual Triad.

Master Djwhal Khul says,

1. Zodiacal energies pass through Shamballa and are related to the first Ray of Will or Power and affect the Monad.

2. Systemic energies pass through the Hierarchy and are related to the second Ray of Love-Wisdom or (as it is oft called

in esoteric astrology) the Ray of Attractive Coherency and affect the soul.

3. Planetary forces impinge upon and pass through humanity and are related to the third Ray of Active Intelligence and affect the personality.[4]

During the time when we are engaged in our triangle work, we can keep in mind the fact that there are many triangular formations of energy in the Universe which are inter-related within greater triangular circulations of force, and within the fiery spheres of energy sources. Through visualizing the triangle participants, we build lines of energy; through invocation we release the energy of Light, Love and Power into these energy lines. Thus, we and many thousands of others on the planet weave a network of triangles through which Light, Love and Power circulate, increasing each day in brightness and intensity.

Humanity lives in this network of Light, Love and Power, and sooner or later touches these triangular electrical lines and receives vision, inspiration and revelation. As humanity's reception increases, it changes its etheric pattern from the square to the triangle, because the trinity of centers listed above contact each other with greater ease and greater attraction, allowing the light to glow as triangles all over its etheric body. As the numbers of triangles increase and include higher centers, man becomes a source of Light, Love and Power; he becomes a path through which others may contact higher visions and higher sources of inspiration.

---

[4]*Ibid.*, p. 411.

Triangle work is not only related to the redemption of humanity; it is also a great service for the great planetary Soul, our Planetary Logos, Who, we are told, is preparing to take a Cosmic Initiation. Thus, we, as the cells of His Body, raise our vibration and help Him carry on His great task on Cosmic levels.

As triangles increase in number and intensity, a greater release of energy will be recorded upon our planet, not only from Hierarchical or Shamballic sources, but from systemic and Cosmic triangles as well.

This inflow of higher energies will create great crises and greater opportunities for human and national units to go forward into greater unity, into greater synthesis — not only with humanity, but also with super-human lives.

As a result of such an alignment, integration and fusion, the seven departments of human endeavor will slowly come under the inspiration of the corresponding Ashrams and Rays. Humanity will witness progress more amazing than any ever witnessed in the history of humanity or the planet.

The enemies of evolution use square patterns to halt the transformation of the planet. In all great breakthroughs, the negative forces reach their highest stage of destructive power. The Hierarchy of Light assumes that such a condition presents greater possibility and opportunity for the advancement of the planet. The greatest opportunity is in the moment of greatest danger, because the dark forces stand in full manifestation and make it easier for the Forces of Light to overcome them and open the path of redemption for all living forms in the Universe. It is only during grave danger that the sword or the lightning of Monadic energy manifests.

The Forces of Light and the forces of darkness are mobilizing themselves. Soon we will reach the midnight hour of civilization, when these two forces are equal in power. It is at that moment that the great Lord will appear, as He told us in the parable of the ten virgins.

It is because of this approaching major crisis that the Hierarchy gave humanity the *Great Invocation*, and the technique of using it in triangular formation, to bring in greater Light, Love and Power, to be ready for the great day of opportunity.

Triangles will eventually create those conditions on Earth in which incoming New-Age souls will effectively work for the Plan. These souls are called the "New Group of World Servers;" their number is continuously increasing. As triangles increase and radiate more Love, more Light and more Power, these New-Age souls will increase in number and will find their right places to work, and have greater opportunity to reveal their beauty, working more effectively in all human affairs without wasting time and energy.

In the esoteric Teaching, we learn that thoughtforms or impressions are transmitted through the etheric body of the planet. This etheric body is like the atmospheric electricity through which thoughts and other impressions travel, as in wireless communication, but from person to person, from center to center. Each person's etheric body is a part of this planetary body, and if our physical body with its nervous and glandular systems is closely connected with the etheric body, then the transmission of these thought currents or impressions reaches the physical brain consciousness easily and without distortion, provided that our etheric body and aura have sufficient purity.

When the fusion of the physical body with the etheric double reaches a certain stage of perfection and our emotions and mental radiations are highly purified and clean, then we register not only thought currents, but also impressions coming from Higher Sources.

In triangle work, the art of building thoughtforms is very important, because it is through our thoughts that we cause changes in the etheric body. Actually, our etheric body is composed of four grades of etheric substance. This substance is like a web, made by tiny streams of energy forming the etheric body.

We can influence change and cause refinement of the etheric body through our ability to think. If we refine our thinking and eventually make our mental vehicle a perfect servant to our Soul impulses and impressions, the etheric body passes through transformation, reconstruction, and gradually the lower etheric substances give way to higher ones, until our whole etheric body is formed by first-grade etheric substance.

As this change progresses in our etheric vehicle, we cause corresponding changes in the etheric body of the planet. That is why by thinking and meditating upon the *Great Invocation*, and by using it, we bring down Hierarchical energies and impressions into our mind, passing them along to our etheric body, then through our etheric body into the etheric body of the planet.

We are told that Christ sounds the *Great Invocation* every day with the entire Hierarchy. "It is used with constancy, exactitude and power." It is very powerful to feel, at the time of saying the Invocation, that we are joined with the Hierarchy as a whole.

By sounding the *Great Invocation*, we not only transform the planetary network and our etheric bodies, but we also help the Plan of the Hierarchy to manifest on Earth. The *Great Invocation* is a perfect summary of the Plan:

- We invoke the increase of light and guidance of the Divine Mind;
- We invoke the revelation of true love in the hearts of men;
- We invoke the reappearance of the Master of angels and men, the Christ;
- We invoke the guidance of Divine Purpose, and the harmonization of the wills of men with Divine Will;
- We invoke divine help to seal the door where evil dwells;
- We invoke the establishment of the Kingdom of God upon Earth.

If we analyze the *Great Invocation*, we see that it reveals the Plan, which is the answer to all our needs.

> Triangles of light,
>
> triangles of goodwill,
>
> triangles of will-to-good

will eventually transform the etheric web of this planet and humanity, bringing into them the Cosmic etheric substance of higher levels. Thus, triangles will evolve into centers through which the Divine Energies of Light, Love and Will are distributed. Through these energies, the Plan will work out, and the Will of God will manifest Itself in a transformed humanity.

Three
Basic
Triangles

*T*here are three basic triangles, which are called:
1. triangles of light;
2. triangles of goodwill; and
3. triangles of will.

1. Triangles of light work mostly with the substance of light, with the fire of mind. Their prime task is to form a triangular etheric formation in the planetary body. They work with the Third Ray, the Ray of intelligence, and they engineer the foundation of the New Age. Their main function is to clear the way for greater power, annihilating glamor from the surface of the planet, and increasing the light of analysis, discrimination and clear thinking.

They use the mantram of Christ, the *Great Invocation,* and through literature, speech and their life example, they organize centers of light — triangles of light which reveal the true Teaching of the Ageless Wisdom. They organize the ways and means to work out the Divine Plan all over the world in very practical ways, such as:

> A. communicating their experience with triangle work to other members of the triangle;

B. spreading information regarding books and articles that demonstrate clear thinking in world affairs, or in any field of human endeavor;

C. organizing meetings where they teach the science of discrimination, analysis and clear thinking;

D. dispelling, as a triangle, the glamors of individuals, groups and nations;

E. using the principle of harmlessness to expose the glamors of the world;

F. revealing the cause of glamor and teaching how to dispel it; and

G. showing the results of glamor in the history of humanity.

Focusing their minds and energies on the above or other related subjects, they render a great service in their environment and for humanity.

In triangle work, we have the cooperation of fire elementals on the mental plane who, seeing the beautiful colors of one's aspiration, cooperate and help him build the triangular formation in Space. They pour their energies into it, and charge it with the magnetism of Higher Spheres.

2. Triangles of goodwill work mostly with Soul energy and with the Second Ray of Love-Wisdom. Their main task is to eradicate illusion which, over-casting the planet, creates separativeness, greed, hatred and fear. They burn away illusion with the fire of the Soul.

This second kind of triangle automatically, naturally uses the network of triangles established by the triangles of light.

The main function of goodwill triangles is to pave the way for the power of the third group, triangles of will. Goodwill is the forerunner of will-to-good. On this level, man knows what will is, what good is, and what purpose is.

These triangles use the mantram of Christ, placing greater emphasis upon the second stanza of the *Great Invocation*. Members of these triangles mostly transmit love-wisdom energy, and actively work for the reappearance of Christ.

All that they do is characterized by "self-forgetfulness, harmlessness and right speech." They use many ways to make their work effective, such as:

A. sending out literature which highlights acts of goodwill from all countries, races and religions, using radio and television to make activities based on goodwill known to all;

B. demonstrating the practical power of goodwill in world affairs, especially in politics, business and religion, encouraging right human relations;

C. organizing meetings where the power of goodwill in all human relationships is discussed, teaching the effect of goodwill upon the physical, emotional and mental health of people, explaining how goodwill brings prosperity, joy and security to humanity;

D. organizing centers of goodwill, where information about world goodwill is distributed in as many languages as possible, and the Plan of the Hierarchy for humanity is revealed;

E. attempting to dispel the illusions of the world by radiating the energy of love-wisdom, forming special meditation groups which mentally dissipate the sin of separativeness;

F. exposing sources of illusion in the world by demonstrating the principle of harmlessness, educating people how to dispel illusion and how to avoid the manufacture of more illusion; and

G. demonstrating through their literature and lectures what illusion does to the health of the human body, the moral health of a nation, and what obstacles toward the progress of the human race it creates.

Thus, triangles of goodwill are healing agents, and agents of education. Their power will increase as days go by, because that power increases in proportion to the elimination of illusion.

3. Triangles of will work mostly with First Ray energy, the Ray of will power, the Ray of government and rulership.

In the past, the lower expression of this Ray was used by powerful personalities; mighty rulers, dictators, commanders and totalitarians came into being.

In the New Age, the higher counterpart of this energy will be used. We will see groups of people acting as rulers, leaders, or even kings, expressing Soul principles to open the way to humanity for world unity and global brotherhood.

Triangles of will pave the way for those groups and mighty individuals who will gradually appear in order to assume their tasks for world redemption. These triangles use the previously established networks of light and goodwill, charging them further with a greater fire — with the fire of Divine Purpose, Divine Will.

Triangles will eventually become so potent that any construction based upon a square pattern will fall apart, and the New Age will be in full sway, because these three triangles will unite humanity, the Hierarchy and Shamballa. The divine circulatory flow, the flow of life, will flow through all Sparks in living form.

Triangles of will also use the mantram of Christ, the *Great Invocation*, but members of this group will focus their attention mostly on the third through fifth stanzas:

> From the centre where the Will of God is known
> Let purpose guide the little wills of men—
> The purpose which the Masters know and serve.

> From the centre which we call the race of men
> Let the Plan of Love and Light work out
> And may it seal the door where evil dwells.

> Let Light and Love and Power restore the Plan on Earth.

Thus, they will form fiery and flaming triangles which will melt away all crystallizations and maya on the path of progress.

> *Maya* is devitalized or redirected by the power of **inspiration**, which is a **form of will energy** accumulated in the Soul. This energy is let loose down the etheric centers, like a burning and healing ray. Through this energy, the

> Soul puts the centers in harmony with the
> rhythm of the great pulsating light of the
> Spark. All centers express psychic energy, and
> *maya* is cleansed because all centers are used
> not by blind urges but by a conscious plan, in
> man and in the universe.[1]

Purification of the human mechanism from glamor, illusion and maya will cause great changes to occur in our health, in social and international relationships, in our culture and civilization, and especially in our spiritual disciplines and progress.

A. Triangles of will will organize centers of education to teach specially qualified people the science of leadership, the science of energy, and the use of will energy for the redemption of humanity.

B. They will hold public classes to teach the science of right human relations. There will be special classes concerning the problems of world leadership and how to help leaders do their best for the welfare of humanity.

C. Their subjective work will be to establish fiery lines of contact between centers on the planet, such as London, New York, Geneva, Darjeeling, Tokyo, and others, making these centers alive with Divine Intent, and with the will-to-unify and synthesize.

D. They will speak about and produce literature regarding right human relations. They will reinforce the endeavors of the triangles of light and goodwill. They will penetrate into political organizations in all nations and shed their wisdom, love and divine leadership upon them.

---

[1] See *The Science of Meditation*, by H. (Torkom) Saraydarian, p. 289.

E. They will organize great meetings in many countries so that the voice of the multitudes is heard by the leaders of nations. They will work with the United Nations for the freedom of all human beings and for the protection of privacy. They will encourage all acts of unity that lead to greater synthesis on a global scale. They will invoke and evoke energy "from the centre where the Will of God is known," and carry this energy, especially at the time of the full moon when zodiacal energies have greater inflow through Shamballa.

F. This group will eventually lead all nations to understand the futility of manufacturing more and producing new destructive weapons, and the futility of making those weapons available to other nations. This group will educate the public to such a degree that no nation will use arms or weapons of any kind against any other nation. They will help us understand that war is ultimate proof that the power of human intellect and judgment is bankrupt. They will use the energy of will, amplified by the energy of Shamballa, the energy of Divine Intent.

G. They will establish true peace on Earth — peace evoked by the will-to-good, which is the will of those disciples who are under the guidance of the Purpose of the great Life of this planet, and oriented toward the highest good.

The work of all three groups of triangles is dedicated to the **service** of humanity, the Hierarchy and Shamballa. It is important to emphasize the word "service" because the function of triangle work is to radiate Light, Love and Power to humanity, which makes the Plan of the Hierarchy more successful, and fulfills the Purpose of the greater Center.

Triangles evoke a tremendous outflow of will energy, not only from Divine Sources, but also from humanity itself. One of the services that triangles provide is to increase will power in humanity, balanced with energies of Light and Love.

4

Goodwill

*A*ccording to the Ageless Wisdom, and according to the observations of psychologists and great thinkers, people have discovered that there is a silent and secret "Core" within man himself that is nothing else but **good**. Thus, they have concluded that man is good in his essential Core, because being a Spark of Almighty Light, Love and Power, he cannot be evil in that Core. Man cannot be dark and criminal, since he is essentially good. No matter what happens to a person or what he does to others, he is still good.

If a person acts in a way we define as criminal, as an expression of evil, or as part of the world of darkness, his Core does not participate in these activities. The person does them because he is hypnotized or hurt; because he is under the pressure of an obsession; or because one or more of his mechanisms — physical, emotional, mental or nervous — are distorted. This is why the original good, the original beauty of the person, is not able to express itself.

For example, when we look at the sky on a stormy day, there may be clouds, rain and a few foggy patches, and we cannot see the sun. We may even think that the sun is not there. But beyond those clouds, beyond all the turbulence, the sun exists, and it is always shining. Because there are obstructive particles in the atmosphere between the world and the sun — between the person and his shining Core of beauty — we cannot see the sun. If the obstruction and turbulence between these two extremes are removed, there is always sunshine — always beauty, goodness and creativity.

The same is true of the human being; man is, from his origin, essentially good. There is no evil in him; there cannot be, because he originates from the great Creative Power, which is Goodness Itself — and he is part of that Power. To be more daring, we may say that man is He; man is that Creative Power.

Sometimes we feel as if the whole exists and nothing else, and that we are part of that whole. Conscious unity with that great whole creates in us a willingness to do good. Acts of goodness make us feel whole, joyful and content. When a person expresses the goodness existing within himself, we say that he is a person of goodwill. Man, in his essence, is all goodness, all beauty. When he begins to express this goodness, this beauty, he becomes a man of goodwill. This process is slow, because every time one tries to contact his inner beauty, his inner goodness, he meets many obstacles.

Obstacles are found within our physical bodies, emotional systems and mental complexities, or they can come to us through friends, newspapers and television, through hatred and jealousy, and through various other avenues which obscure our essential beauty and goodness. For a moment we lose sight of them, but in the end, the sun is always victorious; it eventually disperses the clouds.

The same process occurs within us. When we contact greater beauty within, the source of goodness slowly manifests itself, like a little fountain that grows bigger and bigger until we realize one day that we are the will-to-good itself.

Goodwill is the true expression of the real man. Good is the real man. Goodwill is the outward expression of the radiation of the essential man. Thus we can say that goodwill is the expression of the real man, the real Divinity within man. When we express that beauty in our daily contacts, it corrects many problems in our lives and purifies our whole mode of thinking, feeling and acting. Thus, the real man is in the process of expression. In this way, we touch our inner beauty, our Inner Core.

Goodwill begins to awaken within us as a result of our own suffering, and the awareness of the suffering of others. We see that goodwill is based upon our observation that man can increase his joy, understanding and health, if he increases the joy, understanding and health of others. One cannot say that he is healthy, if he allows everyone around himself to become infected with various diseases. We are discovering in our modern society that a person cannot remain healthy unless he cures his neighbor. If you have a neighbor who is a continual source of germs, how will you remain healthy? Health can be ours only by caring for the health of others.

If we want to increase our joy, understanding and health, we must work to increase and deepen the joy, understanding and health of others. In this way we ignite the radioactivity of goodwill energy, which is latent in the Core of our hearts. Goodwill demands that we think about others a little more than we think of ourselves — just as we should pay extra attention to other cars as we drive on the freeway.

Once an old man was teaching philosophy to his wife. Wanting to joke with him, I asked, "What is the use of this? You will not be able to learn anything more than you already know by teaching her." "On the contrary," he said, "through this course she will have greater insights and ask me many questions, showing me where I am short or wrong. Seeking the answers to her questions will help me to surpass myself."

Making the people around you wiser gives you greater opportunity for self-exertion.

I saw a very beautiful ceremony in a cave in the Middle East. A man walked in, carrying a lighted candle, which he then extinguished. After we sat there for a while in complete darkness, he said, "Can you see what is written on the wall?" We could not see anything, for it was too dark. Then he lit his candle, and then handed out candles to everyone in the cave. As our candles were lit, we were able to see more and more clearly the five-pointed star drawn on the cave wall. He said to us, "In cooperation, we conquer."

By increasing each other's light, joy and health, we increase our own light, joy and health. This is the healthy foundation of families, communities and brotherhoods; it should be the foundation of humanity.

A great teacher once said, "Goodwill is like the flame of a fire; it exists by burning." We exist, our joy exists and our understanding and happiness increase, only when we try to increase these benefits in others. Thus, we can say that a man of goodwill thinks about others a little more than he thinks about himself. This is the solution to many of the problems of mankind.

As I was once visiting the home of a young family, the husband came through the door after work while the wife was sitting with their baby on her lap. Instead of pleasantly greeting us, he walked by us and mumbled, "I am tired. . . ." I said, "John, what kind of hello is that? When you come in go to your wife first of all, kiss her and hug her, throw your baby up in the air and play with him a little. You came in like a cow." "Okay," he said, "what do you want me to do?" "First, kiss your wife and say, 'Honey, I love you.' Now go do it." "Okay," he said. So he went to his wife and gave her a kiss with no fire in it. "No," I said, "that is not the way. Hug her nicely and kiss her, saying, 'I love you; you are so beautiful.'"

It took him a little time to be himself and express his love, but eventually when he played with the baby for a little while and gave his wife a loving kiss, the whole atmosphere of the home changed. Tears came into the eyes of his wife, who said, "See how he has changed!" Psychologically, he had been stuck somewhere. He had become stuck on the freeway of life, and just needed a little help to release his energy of goodwill.

It is a very big key to our success when we realize that goodwill is not just a word, or a box into which we can put our old toys. Goodwill is one of the secret keys to human happiness, joy, understanding and health.

One of the major contributing factors to good health is joy. Joy is the effect produced by the release of good through any kind of expression. Actions of goodwill produce joy, because the energy of goodwill heals the vehicles, eliminating inertia, glamor and illusion.

Any time we stop the flow of goodwill energy, we create over-stimulation, congestion and infection in our physical, emotional and mental natures, creating problems in the corresponding spheres of our social field.

Ill will actually poisons your system. This poison first attacks your glandular system; you begin to feel unhappy; you catch cold easily, and your eyes do not see well. You cannot smile; you cannot digest your food very well, because you are in a bad mood. In Asia it is said that one who is emotionally upset should not eat, because it creates poison. It is better to fast if you are angry, jealous, hateful, or have other negative emotions and attitudes, because whatever you eat will not be well digested. It will create some kind of toxin that will remain in your tissues, emerging later through a complicated illness.

We can say that practicing goodwill is healing, in that it works not only to condition the physical, emotional and mental natures, but it also does **connecting** work. For example, let us say that you have a muddy, dirty swimming pool. If you open a little channel of pure water that flows continuously into the pool, eventually your pool becomes clean. The pure water cleans out the old, dirty, stagnant water, and in time replaces it entirely, until all the water is pure.

The same thing happens in our nature if we open our central energy of good. Man is a coiled energy of good. Once this good starts to radiate, grow and penetrate our whole system, it cleans our mental, emotional and etheric atmospheres so that our bodies can breathe and inhale properly, because we are in good condition.

The bodies are mechanisms. If your etheric, emotional and mental natures are in good condition and energized with the sunlight of your inner good — the Inner Sun — you are really healthy. Your entire system is healthy and you radiate health, instead of germs. A great sage describes how people are greatly concerned about not giving physical germs to others, while giving little consideration to the emotional and mental "germs" that they continuously spread in the forms of depression, negative emotions and negative thoughts.

What happens if you project such germs to your children, your husband or wife, your neighbors, co-workers, and whomever you meet? You are really poisoning their auras. If this continues, you create a polluted atmosphere around yourself and around others, in which health, joy and understanding are impossible.

Life is an opportunity to the person of goodwill. We sometimes forget this.

One day I was riding with a man who was going to sell me a house. "Look," he said very sincerely, "we will be there in ten minutes. If you do not decide in that time to buy it, you will not be able to do so later, because once I leave my car, I know that there are many people waiting there to buy it. Now is the opportunity." "My goodness," I thought. I became very uncomfortable, because the car was driving down the freeway and we were rapidly approaching the house. "Okay," I said, "I will buy it." "I'm glad," he said, "that you are not too late."

It is the same way with life. Life proceeds more rapidly than a car traveling down the freeway. Where are we going? Yesterday we were children, running to our mother. Suddenly, we are old. Before it is too late, we must recognize that life is an opportunity in which we must not lose a single minute. We must try to increase the joy and health of others. And when we are full of goodwill, all the good that we give will return to us hundred-fold. As much as we give, in that proportion we increase the goodwill within ourselves.

There is a poem which expresses this thought very well. It says, "The things that I have given to others are the only things that remain with me — a smile, joy, a gift, compassion." The philosophy of goodwill is nothing but the philosophy of giving.

What is giving? Giving is a process of increasing our radiation. When we give, we do not decrease; we increase because we increase our radiation, power, joy, understanding and health. This process is called giving, but it is really **sharing** with others, more than it is giving.

We must realize that life is very short, and that we must not lose any opportunity to increase the joy, understanding and health of those who are around us, close to us. Karma has brought us together in a way that we influence each other. This is a supreme opportunity that should not be lost. It is too late when we say, "I can do it tomorrow." Tomorrow may never come.

I read a story about a rich man who was giving a wonderful party for his friends. They were happily drinking and eating, when his servant came to him and said, "There is a man waiting for you at the door." The rich man asked, "Who is he?" but the servant did not know. "He seems to be a beggar, sir," he replied. "A beggar?" the rich man exclaimed, heading for the door. When he reached the door and asked the beggar what he wanted, the beggar asked if he could come inside for a while. "My goodness," the rich man said, "I am giving a party now and we are dancing. Please go away and come back tomorrow; I will see what I can do for you then." He closed the door and went back to enjoy the party.

While he was talking with a few of his guests, he suddenly thought, "I should have given that poor man something to eat." The rich man left all his friends at the party to look for the poor beggar and bring him back. But it was too late; the beggar was never found, and the rich man missed an opportunity to share his blessings. That night he dreamed that God visited him and said, "A few hours ago I appeared to you in the form of a beggar, a man who needed food and shelter, but you were too busy with your eating, drinking and partying."

All that is given to you must be shared with those in need, because the real enjoyment of abundance is only experienced through sharing.

When I lived in Van Nuys, there was a German girl working in the post office. She had a very round, cute face; her eyes were dark and almond-shaped, like Chinese eyes, but they always looked very sad, depressed and lonely. One day I said to myself, "I am going to make this girl laugh." So every time I visited the post office, I would stand in line at her window, and try to joke with her. Finally I said to her, "You know, you are pretty." But she turned away.

The next time I went to buy stamps, she started to smile a little. "Look," I said to her, "smile. What is the matter? Sometimes you are like a dark cloud." This made her smile a little more. The next time I visited, I told a little joke that was funny. After that, I made her laugh every time I visited. She used to wait for my visits to the post office to cheer her up and make her feel happy. Sometimes when her line was too long and I could not wait for her, she used to look for me and say a few nice words.

There are many people we can help. We can give them a little release. When we increase the joy of others, we expand not only our own field of radiation, but also the radiation fields of others. This creates an atmosphere in which right human relations, understanding and health become possible.

As goodwill spreads within groups, nations and in the whole of humanity, we will see the elimination of those factors which create misunderstanding, waste, greed, hatred and war. It is only in such an atmosphere of goodwill that humanity as a whole will be able to enter a greater phase of creativity and harmony, and dedicate itself to the exploration of Cosmic possibilities.

Man must think not only about increasing his national joy, understanding and health, but also about increasing global joy, understanding and health. Thus, we will have peace; thus, we will have health and prosperity.

We even dare to say that the health of our planet is conditioned or based upon the active goodwill radiated by each person. The beauty of goodwill is that it is not limited to any one doctrine or dogma. No matter what you believe, no matter in what nation you are born or what religion you observe, you can still exercise goodwill, because in goodness there are no barriers, restrictions, impediments or crystallizations. Goodwill is for all — **good** for all.

We can also say that goodwill is the common denominator for the future unity of humanity, the brotherhood of men and angels. We must exercise goodwill toward ourselves, too. Suppose you performed an act of ill will, or did something wrong in the past. Do not dwell upon it; do not criticize or condemn yourself, poisoning your present life. Instead, minimize or eradicate its effect by increasing acts of goodwill through sacrificial service.

It is possible that every time you want to do good, a past memory of failure or ill will interferes and so you stop the expression of goodwill. Try to release goodness every time you feel its presence within you. Do not let any memory of failure, painful emotion, fear, or separative thought stop you from doing good. Do not let the reactions of others condition the free flow of your goodwill. Goodwill has no expectations, no limitations. It is an energy radiation for all, in spite of any negative attitudes directed your way.

Goodwill is a process by which we flow into the ocean of Love, into the ocean of the Great Presence within all.

Foster Bailey, in writing about goodwill, says:

> The health of the people of the world is one of the pressing problems facing us and the energy of goodwill has healing potency. D.K. says it is effective in curing diseases of the respiratory tract, lungs and throat, the stabilizing of the cells of the brain, the cure of insanities and obsessions, and the attainment of equilibrium and rhythm in daily life.[1]

What Is Goodwill?

The human being has three fundamental powers within himself. His Core is a three-faceted diamond; man is characterized by this diamond. One facet is intelligence; man has the power to search, find, analyze and create. The second facet is love; man has the power to relate, associate, attract and cooperate. The third facet is will-to-good, will power by which man acts, causes change in his environment and controls. These three powers are facets of one diamond.

---

[1]*Beacon*, September-October, 1976, p. 347.

Great thinkers throughout the ages have emphasized how intelligence is destructive if it is not conditioned with love. If there is no love within a person, his intellect will be destructive — even self-destructive. Intelligence makes one successful and creative, and then love shares the success and creative manifestations with others.

In addition to love and intelligence, we must have the will-to-good. Love energy united with intelligence can lack purpose and direction if there is no will power directing it toward higher and higher achievement. Will power directs intelligent activity and loving activity to the purpose of Cosmic power. Without will power, one is not in harmony with the central controlling purpose.

Intelligence creates; love shares whatever intelligence discovers. Love creates relationship and cooperation between people and objects. But it is essential to have will power, so that there is a continuous urge to proceed forward with direction and drive to reach higher and higher levels of achievement.

If these three facets operate together, the person is on the path of perfection. If only one or two of them are in effect, there is a lack of balance. If there is will power without love, the person becomes forceful and totalitarian.

Goodwill is will power directed to God, to the good of all. When goodwill operates in a person, it creates contact between the physical, emotional and mental vehicles, and the person's real Core. This is very important for the development of integrity, energy, and to have influence upon others. If a person is not together, he is divided. When one is divided, he cannot be successful or healthy. He cannot impress others. Goodwill unites the physical, emotional and mental bodies, and then relates them with the Core. In this way, the human mechanism comes under the control of the individual.

There are many states of consciousness in which your physical, emotional and mental bodies are not controlled by you. Other commanders are controlling your thoughts, emotions, glamors, illusions, desires and wishes, making you a divided human being. Goodwill creates total integrity within you, because will power is the Divinity within your heart.

You can awaken goodwill within you by seeing that all beings are travelers toward the Central Core. This is a very essential idea. You cannot have goodwill toward any human being if you do not consider and realize that like you, all human beings are traveling toward the Central Magnet in the Universe; we are all fellow travelers.

In one of His books, M.M. says, "Traveler, let us help each other as we journey through mountains and valleys, through darkness and light, so that we protect each other." When you realize that each human being, no matter who he is, is traveling with you toward that far-distant goal, you also realize that there is a greater possibility that you will meet him at the summit and therefore you are inspired to develop goodwill toward him.

When you realize that your success depends upon the success of others, you begin to develop goodwill. People have a tendency to think that their individual success is separate from the success of others. But if one thinks deeply and experiences more deeply, he will see that no man can be successful by himself. For example, if people did not cooperate, you would not have any clothing to wear, books, schools, cities. Everyone in the world helps you have all that you have. You cannot live alone.

If the people around you are successful, it is likely that you will be more successful because of their success. For example, if you are rich and open a big market in a poor village, you will most likely go bankrupt. But if you open a big market in a place where people are successful, it is more likely that you will succeed. Goodwill tries to make other people successful.

Suppose you are a scientist and everybody around you is ignorant. How can you actualize your discoveries? What good are they if no one understands them? But if you find people who can think and create, you will be successful and productive.

Your success depends upon the success of others. Your success depends upon the health, intelligence, love and goodness of other people. If they do not have intelligence, love and goodwill, you are not going to be successful, because eventually they will bring you down.

A very important realization to develop is that we cannot be successful unless we are surrounded by successful people, or if we do not make the people around us successful, rich, creative, healthy and prosperous. When we think this way, we develop goodwill toward others, because their existence becomes essential to our own existence and well-being.

Let us say that you are building a house and you have no tools or helpers to help you build it. You cannot build that house because you need materials and tools that have been made by other people.

Jealousy, separatism and self-interest have no place in our lives. Jealousy says, "I must be prosperous, no one else." Such a person cuts his own throat. When a person eventually destroys the sense of separatism within himself, from that moment on goodwill develops in him. As long as the sense of separatism exists within us, we cannot cultivate goodwill.

Essentially, Good is God. Divine Will is in every creature, and because Divine Will and Divinity are one within us, we develop a sense of unity and cooperation. Groups are created to exercise group consciousness, group unity and group oneness to help others to succeed. If members of a group are separative to each other, if they hate each other and are jealous or revengeful toward each other, this divides the consciousness of the group and unity dissolves. The same conditions happen in families, nations and humanity.

What Goodwill Does.

1. Goodwill heals the body. Scientists and doctors are discovering that if the mind is really together, functioning without cleavages, it can heal the body. Unity, oneness and integrity of the mind cannot exist without a unified consciousness. Consciousness can never be unified without will power behind it to sustain it.

It is will power that regenerates and heals your system. Will power comes from the innermost Core of your being. We can say that will power is the manifestation of the Divinity that exists within you.

2. Goodwill purifies the emotions and creates integrity and health in the emotional body. We have been so preoccupied with our physical body for millions of years that we still have very little idea what the emotional body is. We will soon discover that the emotional body is identical to the physical organism. It needs care. For example, hatred, anger, revenge, jealousy and fear are all sicknesses in the emotional body, just as cancer or a tumor is a sickness in the physical body. But will power filled with goodness can purify your whole emotional system, creating in it aspiration toward the Common Good.

If you hate someone and are really angry at him, take a moment and set your goodwill into operation. Imagine yourself taking him a gift. Imagine meeting him at his home, hugging him and talking nicely with him. Imagine that he gives you a gift and that you have a wonderful conversation. When you do this, you will see your hatred and malice evaporate — because you are putting goodwill into operation.

3. Goodwill also purifies and energizes your mental mechanism. Just like electricity, it charges your battery and suddenly your engine is working.

I had a typewriter that I had not used in many years. I switched it on, and it took several minutes to become sensitive to my fingertips. Half an hour later, it started to type out a few characters. I saw that the letters were not hitting well, because the electricity had not penetrated fully enough. After two hours, the electricity was able to charge the whole machine, and it began to operate at full capacity.

It is the same with the energy of goodwill. When you turn it on, it starts to operate your physical, emotional and mental bodies, making them more sensitive and productive.

4. Goodwill not only heals, but it also builds communication lines, electrical lines between the physical, emotional and mental bodies and the Central Core, which pumps energy into these systems like the heart pumps blood into the arteries.

Without goodwill, you are an abyss. Every kind of destruction that occurs in the world is from the absence of goodwill.

Have you noticed how something changes in the atmosphere when Christmas comes? This is because more people try to exercise goodwill by giving gifts to each other, sending cards with best wishes and love, or telephone calls, telegrams saying, "How are you? I miss you," and so on. This energy changes the atmosphere, because more people are exercising goodwill.

The energy of goodwill brings right human relations. If you will good toward another person, you will have right relations with that person. Right human relations are streams of energy that pour out from goodwill.

What would happen if we had right human relations worldwide? We would not be subjected to heavy taxation; there would be no wars or war expenditures, no exploitation, no killing. The money spent correcting and supplying these endeavors would stay in our own pockets to be used creatively. We could use the money to annihilate hunger and poverty, build art and science centers, beautify and clean the whole world.

Goodwill is the only practical way to bring humanity together and create abundance. For example, let us take two nations at war with one another. For many years they have been killing each other and destroying each other's property. If you calculate how much money both sides spent and how many thousands of people were lost, you will realize the heavy cost of ill will.

We know of the emotional tensions between nations, various groups and churches. The Catholics and Protestants are killing each other, bombing each other, and so on. These emotional tensions evaporate the moment that people think of each other as co-travelers on the path toward one God. Instead of spending our money and energy creating ammunition and hatred, we could extend a little goodwill and make life more productive and less expensive.

5. The energy of goodwill works for the health and survival of humanity. We can see very clearly that unless goodwill is established among nations, this planet is not going to survive. If the "super-powers" do not extend goodwill to one another, all nations are endangered. Even the animal and vegetable kingdoms are threatened, because we are poisoning everything on the planet. Only goodwill energy will save humanity and the planet.

6. Goodwill secures the health of the planet. I was reading an article about the rain forests, which stated that seventy-five percent of these forests is endangered. We are using Nature as a source of exploitation and not relating to Her with goodwill; we think we can do anything to Her and escape the consequences. But because Nature is our Mother, our source of nourishment, if we kill Her, we will not survive. Only goodwill toward our Mother will allow Her to survive, and when She survives, we survive.

7. Goodwill creates equilibrium and balance. Earthquakes, tornadoes, and other calamities on the planet and in the solar system, are the result of disturbances in Space which are caused by ill will. If thousands of people with ill will accumulate in one place, it is assured that there will be great earthquakes in that area. That is why great disciples are sent to act as shock absorbers in those places that are polluted with ill will.

There is the story in the Old Testament where the angel came to Lot and agreed not to burn Sodom and Gomorrah if he could find ten righteous men. But Lot could not find that many righteous men and so the cities were burned.

8. Goodwill repairs what is created by the disturbances in Space. In Space there are lots of storms, solar winds, electromagnetic storms and vast tidal waves that reach our planet after a solar system or galaxy has been annihilated or burned. For example, if a galaxy suddenly disappears, it creates a great vacuum, which then starts a tidal wave. These kinds of tidal waves travel through Space and create disturbances in other solar systems, including our own. But if we have goodwill here, it protects us and creates harmony in the area of our planet and solar system.

We can see what great power and creativity were exhibited in the lives of those great geniuses in history who were filled with the energy of goodwill. Goodwill creates a magnetic field around them which attracts high-level ideas and visions from centers of Light in the Universe, making their labor a glorious symphony. The greater the amount of goodwill a genius has, the greater good he can do for humanity.

Many artists and creative people observe that whenever they do something against goodwill, against the good of others, their inspiration evaporates. You can observe this in your own life. You will see that if you are playing a musical instrument, or writing during a moment of inspiration, or really excited with a vision, the moment you bring any degree of ill will into your system, you will see how your inspiration dies out and your creativity stops.

There was a girl who was the most beautiful singer. One day while she was performing, one of her old boyfriends came in. She began to lose control; eventually, she turned red and became nervous, and left the stage. Later I asked her, "Why did all your inspiration, the beauty of your voice, the song and everything you were radiating, suddenly vanish?" She said, "Because I hate him. I did not want to see his face." This was a great example to me of what happens when a person short-circuits his electrical system with ill will. Ill will is anti-survival.

What Ill Will Does.

1. Ill will creates sickness. When you wish ill for others, you poison your own system. By looking at the faces of people, you can see this. A face filled with goodwill shines. There is a smile on it; there is health and blessing in it; there is peace. But if a person is full of ill will, his face will change; an ugly look comes into his eyes; his whole body is different.

One day I went to visit a man who was one hundred and seven years old. I asked him, "What is your secret for living so long?" He said to me, "Longevity depends on your heart." "Yes," I said, "the heart is a very important organ in the body." "That is not what I mean," he said. "If there is goodwill in your heart, you will live longer. I survived and became victorious in life only because I exercised goodwill whenever I faced an obstacle."

He told me a story of a trip he took through the mountains in winter. At one point he was surrounded by hungry wolves. Instead of running, he sat down and talked with them, saying, "You can eat me if you must, but I am all bone. It will not satisfy you. Wolf brothers, do not eat me; you will find more appropriate food." The old man said that the wolves left him in peace because he loved them.

Goodwill creates protection; it is the only language spoken by every life-form. You can speak goodwill to trees, animals, to your pets — even to your enemies. All of them understand the language of goodwill.

2. Ill will destroys friendship. If a person starts thinking of self-interest and evil, his friendships evaporate. Goodwill creates friendship because it is love plus action, inclusiveness, direction and purpose. Ill will poisons all relationships. You suddenly tire of a person because you see ill will in him. When there is ill will, the relationship is poisoned; separatism is created, weakening the relationship and any efforts of action, preventing higher contact with Higher Forces, eventually dissolving the relationship.

Christ says that if you are going to give a gift to God or offer a prayer to Him, you should first make peace with all your enemies. There is something very deep in this instruction. If you do not have peace between you and your enemy, you cannot make contact with God because of these disturbances. Some people claim that God speaks to them and tells them to kill others, but the real God would never ask a person to kill a child of His.

Avoid all activities that are not based upon goodwill. If you have a friend or a partner who wants to go into business with you, or who wants to marry you, observe whether or not he exercises goodwill. If that person does not have goodwill, you would be building your house upon the sand. If you see that he demonstrates goodwill, it is likely that your business or relationship will be very successful. All our disappointments and failures are based upon ill will.

Avoid any conversation or written expression that is charged with hatred, fear, anger, malice, jealousy, slander or separatism. These increase ill will in the world. Do not read books that are filled with heavy hatred, separatism, anger, treason or slander. If you and your children read such books, you will be poisoned with ill will. You cannot expect the next generation to create goodwill and right human relations under such circumstances.

When you are in the current of negative thinking and really charged with ill will, it is like riding on the back of a wild horse of hatred, malice and slander. You cannot stop that horse immediately, but try to see if you can stop the thoughts that are charged with ill will. By doing so, you are becoming a victorious human being; you have just started to become human. If you practice this, you will see in just a few months how your health improves, because goodwill is healing.

Many people are charged with slander, malice, hatred, jealousy and fear through our magazines, television and movies. We are surrounded by these things. But if you fill your soul with the energy of goodwill, it builds a shield around you so that the surrounding ill will does not penetrate into your heart. A great Master says in one of His writings, "Protect the heart, because the river of Life pours from the heart." For example, if fifty people around you are poor, make yourself rich enough to give to them. Instead of their sickness and weakness affecting you, you affect them with your beauty. You cannot control or change them, but you can change and control yourself.

Sometimes you listen to people who are gossiping about others, and you are drawn into their conversation and gossip. When this happens, you often feel so defeated afterwards. But if you keep awake and increase your goodwill, you will eventually resist such conversations. It takes a lot of exercise to do this, but it is worth it.

To have goodwill does not mean to be exploited or manipulated by others. Being a person of goodwill does not mean that you serve the vices, glamors, illusions and hatreds of others. Your goodwill must be used to awaken and cultivate goodwill in others, even with disciplinary actions and soberness, if necessary.

Remember that there are three ways to develop goodwill. The first is to have a contact with your innermost Self through meditation and prayer. Sometimes through ecstasy in a great success or in a moment of great inspiration, you suddenly contact your Self, and that fills your heart with goodwill.

When I was a young man, I really hated several people who lived in the same monastery. One day I traveled twenty-two thousand feet up into the mountains. As I looked down, it was so beautiful that I started to cry. When I returned from the trip to the monastery, I approached the people I had once hated and hugged them; I loved them. When they asked, "What happened?" I answered, "It was so beautiful!" In that beauty, no ill will could exist.

The second way is to realize that everybody is a traveler toward the Central Core. Third, you must recognize the presence of God in all human beings.

If you want to increase your own goodwill, try to control your actions, speech, feelings and thoughts so that they do not express ill will.

If you want to destroy a person, encourage him to gossip. A person who gossips will eventually turn pale; the gracefulness, the smile and beauty will leave his face. If you want to save a person, inspire him with goodwill by your own example of generosity, nobility, honesty, beauty and joyfulness.

We had a neighbor whom we disliked very much. It was Christmas time and my mother told us that we were going to fast during Christmas, at a time when we usually dined well. We could not believe that we were going to have to fast. But my mother insisted. We fasted for five days. My mother took the money that was not spent on food because of our fasting, and went to the store. She returned with food and presents for the neighbor, who was also poor. "What is this?" the neighbor asked. "Well," my mother said, "I thought you might need some of these things for the holy days." "What about you?" she said. "I don't care about us; we care about you." The woman cried and cried, saying "How can you do this for me?" Later when she found out that five people in our family fasted during Christmas for her sake, she kissed my mother's feet and said, "I am sorry from now on." The cleavage was totally healed.

This is just one way to inspire goodwill; you can create many different ways. But whatever way you choose, it must be charged with goodwill. Only then will your attempts be successful.

Meditation

You may do the following meditation for five to ten minutes each day at sunset.

1. Relax and calm your emotions and thoughts, and say:

   O Self-Revealing One, reveal Thyself in me.

2. OM   OM   OM

3. Visualize the sun, pouring its light upon you, purifying your etheric body, your emotional nature and your mental nature.

4. See yourself standing in the light, radiating as a transfigured being.

5. Meditate on the following seed thought:

    The future of the world lies in the hands
    of men and women of goodwill.

6. In your imagination, raise your hands and bless the whole world, sending peace, love and hope to all.

7. Repeat the *Great Invocation*.

8. OM   OM   OM

5

Psychological Effects Of The Use Of The Great Invocation

*M*any millions of men and women feel helpless regarding current world conditions; they feel that all is futile. They have a great sense of value, justice and freedom, but for many reasons they cannot exercise their own will to cause the changes which need to be made, and they fall into depression and frustration.

The teaching of the *Great Invocation* gives us great hope and steady courage. In focusing the mind and repeating the Invocation, we **can** cause great changes in world affairs. Groups organized to repeat the *Great Invocation*, both large and small, feel new enthusiasm and joy when they see changes occurring toward the betterment of social life. They see that they are contributing to these changes, rendering service to their nation and humanity. And as they continue in their endeavors to sound the *Great Invocation* and to form new triangles, their interest in world affairs increases tremendously. Gradually the participants emerge from inertia and enter the field of active social work. They see the power of thought; they see the power of love and goodwill; they see the power of optimism and the power of will-to-good.

There are many thousands of men and women actively engaged in the task of spreading the *Great Invocation* and increasing triangles all over the world, in all countries. Such a mental attitude produces peace, optimism and healthy relationships, thus helping to build a better world in which to live.

It is of deep significance that the *Great Invocation* is used by people of faiths other than Christian. The recognition of the fundamental spiritual unity of the whole human family under one God — making all men brothers — is growing. It transcends false attitudes of superiority and refutes prejudice and condemnation which adversely affect human relations. The worldwide use of the *Great Invocation* is a great step forward in the cause of world brotherhood and, therefore, in the cause of world stability and peace.

The healing of nations begins by increasing hope and vision within each individual, causing him to feel that he can help change the condition of humanity by working primarily through his mental body, creating constructive thoughtforms which spread joy, gratitude and beauty, and which evoke goodwill and right human relations.

I remember an eighty-four-year-old man who was living in a retirement home. He told me that he was waiting to die. After I introduced him to the use of the *Great Invocation* and spoke about the effects that it could produce in the world, he accepted it. A few months later when I visited him again, his room looked like a business office. He was distributing the *Great Invocation* not only in his area, but all over the country, receiving very encouraging letters, letters of gratitude and letters filled with questions.

"How are you doing?" I asked him. "Oh, my goodness," he replied, "I am so busy packing and addressing cards printed with the *Great Invocation*, and trying to answer all these questions! If only God would grant me a few more years, I could do more organized work."

This was a man who had been waiting to die, secluded in his room in depression, feeling a deep sense of futility. The *Great Invocation* not only restored his faith in the future of humanity, but it also increased his will to live and to serve.

I am certain that many thousands of people have had similar experiences. The *Great Invocation* changes despair into hope, inertia into courage, and makes a person work for the Common Good of humanity.

When we repeat the *Great Invocation*, it evokes protection and Soul guidance. The energy of the Inner Guide begins to flow into our personality. It is even possible that energy from higher centers and from the Great Ones flows into us and into our environment when we repeat it.

Aspiration is an effort to surpass any level which limits us. It is an effort to enter a greater field of spiritual satisfaction. Through the *Great Invocation*, we tune ourselves in with greater centers of Light, Love and Power in the Universe:

Center of Light	Lord Buddha,
Center of Love	Christ, and
Center of Will	Sanat Kumara;

with the:

Lords of Liberation,
Avatar of Peace, and
Avatar of Synthesis;

and with:

Sirius,
the Pleiades, and
the Great Bear.

Master Djwhal Khul, in speaking about the esoteric side of triangle work, says:

> . . . Masters from the various Ashrams made a decision to work . . . in order to bring order out of chaos by pouring into the planetary astral plane pure astral energy, untainted by glamour and revelatory of pure love.[1]

He also says:

> [T]his pure astral energy, directed under law into our planetary life, is free from all that is at present associated with the astral plane: glamour and delusion, emotional fog and poisonous deceiving phenomena.[2]

Some Masters Who tread the path of higher evolution transfer this energy into the Hierarchy and humanity. Master Djwhal Khul, referring to the *Old Commentary*, explains the technique in the following way:

> The Master throws Himself — under the liberating Law of Sacrifice — into the vortex of the astral life of the One to Whom our Lord relates Himself with humble joy. And as the Master works, there forms before His eyes a triangle of force in shades of varying rose. By His magnetic power, He concentrates the energy required. Then through this triangle of

---

[1]Bailey, Alice A., *The Rays and The Initiations*, p. 402.
[2]*Ibid.*, p. 401.

force, as through an open door, He sends the potency of love into our planet, and till His cycle ends He thus must work.[3]

The work of the triangles organized by Master Djwhal Khul in 1937, was intended:

> . . . to facilitate the work of distributing the pure incoming love energy (expressing itself as light and as goodwill) into the Hierarchy and Humanity.[4]

This pure energy will eventually transmute the substance in which humanity lives, thus providing a pure sphere of love and light in which the function of the Hierarchy will be possible, with all its power and wisdom.

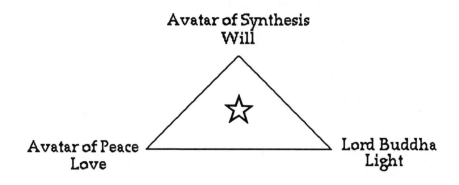

[3]*Ibid.*, p. 402.
[4]*Ibid.*

There is another very potent triangle which is formed by the Avatar of Synthesis, the Avatar of Peace, and Lord Buddha. We are told that Christ stands at the center of this triangle, as the Dispenser of more abundant Life, and channels this threefold energy for the transformation of life for coming centuries.

These three great sources of energy transmit the energy of will power and synthesis, the energy of love and attraction, the energy of light and intelligence.

It is through these energies that humanity will gradually enter the greater light of understanding and cooperation, the greater sphere of loving energy, the greater sphere of Divine Will. Thus, as a conductor of energies, Christ will eventually bring beauty out of chaos, unity out of separatism, creativity out of destruction.

> [T]he . . . outpouring potency of the Christ will be so great that the distinction between love and hate, between aggression and freedom, and between greed and sharing will be made lucidly clear to the eyes and minds of all men. . . .[5]

In speaking about Christ, the Tibetan Master says:

> The Christ is working . . . in very close cooperation with the Master Morya, and also with the Manu (one of the three Heads of the Hierarchy), and these three — the Christ, the Manu and the Master Morya — create a triangle of energies into which (and through which)

---

[5]Bailey, Alice A., *The Reappearance of the Christ*, p. 111.

the energy of the Avatar of Synthesis can pour, finding right direction under Their combined efforts.[6]

In saying the *Great Invocation*, man surpasses his little self, and, like a radio, tunes in to these tremendous frequencies. If his contact is continuous, and if the flow of energy is received, absorbed and assimilated, then man becomes a really conscious transmitter of the energies of Light, Love and Power, and he helps in the transformation of the planet.

While you invoke, put your will power behind the words, and with deep concentration, trust that you are creating a sacred contact. Then the energy will follow your thought.

---

[6]Bailey, Alice A., *The Externalisation of the Hierarchy*, p. 663.

6

How Triangles Work

A man is a point of energy in the etheric body of the planet. Using thought energy, he causes the flow of etheric energy. There is the saying that, "Energy follows thought."

By visualizing three points of energy in Space and projecting lines of energy between these three points, we build a triangle through which the energy of mental fire — or light, the energy of buddhic fire — or love, and the energy of atmic power — which is will, circulate, forming an established triangular pattern of energy. Actually, this kind of work bisects square patterns and produces triangles.

As triangles increase in quantity and in intensity, they bring in higher energies to the three worlds of human endeavor, and a greater energy inflow into the planetary body and into our social system.

The average man builds a very faint triangular formation. Advanced disciples who know how to use visualization and creative imagination build more radiant and stable triangular formations.

Great Initiates build these triangular formations as beams of light through which Their love, wisdom and power precipitate. But no matter on which level a person is found, he helps the overall process by constructing triangles. Eventually, when his triangle makes contact with other triangles, he himself receives more light, and his triangle is charged with greater light. This network of triangles gradually absorbs the energy of goodwill, which expresses itself as right human relations.

Triangular formations are built by streams of thought charged with the quality of Love and Divine Purpose. Such a formation naturally attracts energy which is constructive and in harmony with Divine Intent. That is why this energy is called the energy of goodwill.

It is only this kind of energy which creates right human relations, relationships based upon the foundation of Light, Love and Power. When we express greater light, understanding, knowledge and vision in our lives, with greater love for our fellowman, inspired by examples of great sacrificial servers, with greater dedication, endurance and power, we cause great changes — not only within ourselves, but also within those with whom we come in contact on physical, emotional and mental levels.

Triangular Patterns.

A triangle is a pattern through which energy can flow more easily than it can between the angles of a square. It is a stronger form of construction than the square. When the ancients built the pyramids, they chose the triangular formation. It has now been proven that a pyramid is a powerful transmitter of energy.

It is not only possible to build triangles, but also to build pyramids. One disciple stands on the apex and forms four triangles as the sides of his pyramid. This requires five people. Numbers 1, 2 and 5 form one triangle and one side of the pyramid; numbers 2, 5 and 3 form another triangle and side; numbers 3, 5 and 4 form another triangle and side; and numbers 4, 5 and 1 form the last triangle and side. There are now four triangles. Person number 5 will sound the *Great Invocation*, while visualizing four triangles and the four other people. Numbers 1 through 4 will each visualize two triangles, and say the *Great Invocation*. This will increase the power of the triangles tremendously. Five people form a pyramid — and also symbolize the five-pointed star.

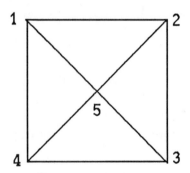

It is very beneficial if the apex of the pyramid is a First Ray soul who can remain firm at the inflow of energy from the etheric body of the planet. Distribution is then carried out by the other triangles, the composition of which can be Second or Third Ray souls, or perhaps personalities.

This method of visualization must not be exercised until triangular visualization proceeds easily and naturally.

In reading the writings of Master Djwhal Khul, we see that there is a pyramid in the Hierarchy Itself, the apex of which is Christ. The four points of the triangles are held respectively by Master M., Master K.H., the Manu, and

Master R. Christ is also the center of a triangle formed by the Avatar of Synthesis, the Avatar of Peace, and Lord Buddha (see diagram in Chapter 5).

Master Djwhal Khul says that Christ sounds the *Great Invocation* every day. We can visualize Him as being present at the midpoint of our triangles. This will give us greater confidence, and create a greater flow of energy into our triangles.

The pattern of the triangle is the original pattern of the circulation of the energies of the soul. It is also a reflection of the Spiritual Triad within which the energies of pure Light, pure Love and pure Will Power circulate and radiate.

The etheric network of the previous solar system was a network of squares. This pattern, which heavily influenced all areas of human endeavor, was inherited in our solar system. The previous solar system worked solely on the perfection of the personality, which is a square consisting of: a) the lower mind; b) the emotional body; c) the etheric body; and d) the physical body.

This solar system is related to soul values, the pattern of which is triangular. We have the Chalice of the Soul formed by twelve petals, each tier representing three petals of energy, called knowledge, love and sacrifice petals.

The next solar system will be a system of concentric circles in which the Solar Life will reach solar perfection in His manifestation.

By increasing triangles and releasing the energies of Light, Love and Power, we help ourselves and humanity enter into the path of true freedom, true simplicity and true beauty. Simplicity is the gift of increasing Light. Freedom is the gift of increasing Love; beauty is the gift of increasing

Light, Love and sensitivity to the Plan and Purpose. Only through increasing Light will humanity enter an age of simplicity. Freedom is the virtue of those who know how to love; it is only in Love that freedom will find its true nature and usefulness.

We are told that Christ links the heart center of this planet with Sirius, from which radiate the energies of Love and the Laws of Freedom. He also links humanity with the Hierarchy, thus forming another triangle. Those who work in triangles eventually realize that such work has limitless potential in all departments of human endeavor.

A. Triangle work links various types of people and puts them in subjective communication. It expands people's consciousness and viewpoints, and even expands their field of information. It links many lower and higher levels together; the lower receives inspiration from the higher, the higher sees more clearly the needs and problems of the lower. Such a relationship eventually brings different levels, races, nations, viewpoints, sources of knowledge and wisdom closer together. Thus, synthesis slowly emerges out of the chaos of separative tendencies.

B. Triangle work not only brings people closer together, but it opens channels of inflowing energy from the Great Ones to humanity. The Great Ones are points of Light, streams of Love and sources of Power. As humanity approaches the Great Ones, the threefold energies of Light, Love and Power pour down into humanity and change not only the patterns of circulation in the human etheric vehicle, but they also inspire greater striving in mankind toward world unity, improvement of life, and deeper penetration into the heart of the laws and principles of the Universe.

This kind of striving to communicate with sources of greater inspiration leads to changes in our culture.

C. Triangle work literally provides increased inspiration to those who have any artistic talent. The interesting point is that those who are inspired by the released energy of triangles not only express deeper creativity, but their work suggests world unity, the betterment of life as a whole, and the conservation of natural resources. Their work reflects not only a desire for perfection of the human heart, but it also expresses the creativity of the artist in the most energizing, sublimating and transforming words, colors, forms, music and movement, building a bridge of achievement for all those who contact their inspirational works.

D. Working to communicate with Higher Sources brings moral upliftment to those who work in our political, social, economic, religious, medical and legal fields, gradually eliminating dishonesty, bribery, exploitation and selfish interest. The sense of responsibility urges a person to purify his motives and to render honest service to his fellowman, without misusing his power, knowledge or position, and without serving selfish interests.

Moral upliftment is the result of contacting higher energies, higher visions and the Plan of the Hierarchy. When a person experiences such upliftment, he alters his life so that it becomes an instrument of service, a bridge of achievement, a torch of enlightenment. He ceases to use other people for his own self-serving purposes, or for his glamors and illusions. This is how right human relations are created, when people turn to each other with the power of goodwill and understanding.

Triangle work will eventually achieve such a goal. Each triangle will be an agent which uplifts its environment. When the number of triangles increases to several million, a great network of Light, Love and Power will work as a powerful transmitter of healing and uplifting energies.

E. The healing of nations will come from Higher Sources. These Sources are active on higher planes, such as the Intuitional and Atmic Planes. Triangles consist of lines of fusion with such Sources.

As triangles increase in number and power, disease will slowly decrease. Illness is the result of mal-circulation of energy. When the divine circulatory flow breaks through obstacles, hindrances and impediments existing in living forms, illness will vanish, and good health with all its blessings will be ours.

Triangles provide a link with healing energies. They encourage us to put our house into order; they help us clean our mechanism and open the path for the free circulation of energy within our mental, emotional, physical and moral natures.

F. Building triangles of light leads to understanding the value of economy. Wasted energy is misused energy. Misused energy produces results which are not in our best interest. Misused energy eventually leads the individual mechanism into disorder. Many people have more energy than they know how to use properly; many others do not have enough energy, because they do not know how to acquire it, or they do not care to strive for it. Wasted energy, as well as greed, possessiveness, and a desire for more than we can use positively, create polluted air, water and soil. We are now paying for our foolishness with ill health.

Triangles of light will lead us to gradual detachment from greed by helping us to understand the Law of Economy — the law of not wasting. When a new spirit of economy is worldwide, we will stop polluting our sources of life. Economy means directing energy to the right purpose without misusing it for glamor, illusion or greed.

One effect of triangles is that the urge-to-have will become the urge-to-be. We will recognize that happiness, joy and success are not based upon what one has — but upon what one is.

G. Triangle work will bring in the Aquarian Age. A new age does not come about by itself; people bring in a new age. It is true that each different age, such as the Piscean Age or the Aquarian Age, brings in different types of energy than the energy of the previous age. But if humanity cannot respond to the new energies with a higher, sublimated and transformed nature, these energies become degenerative factors in the lives of nations and humanity. There is no light for one who is blind, even if you increase the intensity of light before his eyes.

If a small percentage responds to the new energies while the majority does not, the majority — which is of a lower nature — will be stimulated in its lower nature, and it will overcome and destroy all that was created by the small minority of advanced individuals who were able to use the new energies properly.

Master Djwhal Khul gave us the teaching of triangles to help us prevent such a disaster. Triangle work is an endeavor to convert the square patterns of the undeveloped, material or inhuman man, into triangular formation, thus making him sensitive to New-Age energies, visions and revelations.

Once a person begins to respond to New-Age energies, he will put his house in order with his own hands and feet, and will not become a problem or burden to society.

The New Age is the age of group consciousness. The formation of a triangle is the first unit of a group. Group consciousness is the awareness that all life is related, that man does not live only for himself.

H. Triangle work paves the way for the externalization of the Hierarchy and the reappearance of Christ — the real Aquarius. Each time masses of people recite the *Great Invocation* in triangular formation, they evoke Light, Love and Divine Guidance. They establish greater and closer communication with:

1. the center of Light;
2. the center of Love;
3. the center of Power;
4. the Plan;
5. the Purpose;
6. the Hierarchy; and
7. Christ.

They release energy which emanates from such communications into the "center which we call the race of men," to "seal the door where evil dwells."

Many people think that evil does not exist. Evil is an urge to commit crime against mankind and Nature. To "seal the door where evil dwells" is to eliminate those causes which prevent the evolution of mankind, which in turn cause man to suffer. Whether these causes are in man or in Nature, they are activated by wrong attitudes and ignorance.

At this time, the *Great Invocation* is the greatest aid to humanity. The fulcrum, the axis of the *Great Invocation*, is Christ — the reappearance of the great Lord, Christ.

Great Teachers, such as H. P. Blavatsky, Master Djwhal Khul, and Master M., tell us that Christ is a living individual, a living human being Who, because of His unparalleled progress, became the Head of the Hierarchy. He will hold that position for another two thousand years.

We are told that He is presently living in a very isolated spot in the Himalayas, serving humanity on various planes of existence. Thousands of people have contacted Him as they passed through their first and second initiations.

Some people like the *Great Invocation* because of its vision and power, but they do not like to use the word "Christ." They give themselves permission to change the *Great Invocation*, which was not originated by them. Changing or deleting the Name of Christ eliminates the focus of the energies. It can even be harmful to those who use the *Great Invocation* for their personal or group advantages.

Mantrams are like chemical or geometrical formulas; changing one word gives the mantram an entirely different result, or makes it misleading, dangerous or useless. Mantrams are transmitters of energy. When the transmitter is not constructed in a particular order, the energies can be destructive or negative, creating confusion and chaos in the subtle planes of human endeavor. Many mental disorders are the result of a misuse of prayers, mantrams and chanting. Let us not forget that the Hierarchy uses the *Great Invocation* in its original form every day.

Those who, with good intentions, want to change the *Great Invocation*, would do better to create a totally different invocation of their own — instead of distorting a master-piece painting with their unskilled brush.

The most important and powerful line of the *Great Invocation* is:

May Christ return to Earth.

Curiously enough, it is this line which is under attack. By changing this formula, the *Great Invocation* no longer exists. This is what the distorters want.

Master Morya, in speaking about Christ, says:

> One may build a city, one may give the best knowledge, but most difficult of all is to reveal the true Image of Christ. Think, how to cleanse the Image of Christ.
>
> Gathering the crumbs of the people's concept of the Savior and replacing the chiton by overalls, one can find illumination.
>
> By human hands must the Temple be built.[1]

When you are voicing,

May Christ return to Earth,

put all your aspiration and heart into your voice, visualizing at the same time that you are expressing the aspirations of a great number of people.

Another expression which is misunderstood by many is:

And may it seal the door where evil dwells.

---

[1]Agni Yoga Society, *Leaves of Morya's Garden*, Vol. II, p. 75.

Master Djwhal Khul explains this passage very clearly in the following way:

> ... The evil referred to has nothing to do with the evil inclinations, the selfish instincts and the separativeness found in the hearts and minds of human beings. These they must over-come and eliminate for themselves. But the reduction to impotency of the loosed forces of evil which took advantage of the world situa-tion, which obsessed the German people and directed the Japanese people, and which worked through barbarity, murder, sadism, lying propaganda and which prostituted sci-ence to achieve their ends, requires the imposi-tion of a power beyond the human. This must be invoked and the invocation will meet with speedy response. These evil potencies will be occultly "sealed" within their own place. . . .[2]

As we sound this verse, we are also reminded to seal the door of our individual evils, those hindrances which pre-vent the expansion of our consciousness, the expansion of our service and contact with higher centers of Light, Love and Power.

There is another very important formula in the *Great Invocation*:

> *Let purpose guide the little wills of men —*
> *The purpose which the Masters know and serve.*

---

[2]Bailey, Alice A., *The Externalisation of the Hierarchy*, pp. 489-490.

Let us remember that Divine Will is the Power which stands behind all purpose. Purpose is manifested, formulated will, in time and space. Will is the power from which purpose originates, varying according to the cycle and need. Purpose is a partial will. When the cycle changes and when the purpose is fulfilled, that purpose no longer exists.

Let us take a very simple example. Your purpose is to go to New York. Your plan is to travel by airplane. When you reach New York, you no longer need the airplane, nor the original purpose, because you have now fulfilled your purpose by following your plan. You may now conceive a new purpose and a plan, but Will stands forever; It exists forever.

Suppose you are a king, and your will is to have a palace. The palace is your purpose. Architects translate it into a plan. Then the programming starts, and people figure out how to build it. When the palace is built, the purpose has been accomplished; it is over. But the will of the king can create another purpose.

Will is the power to decide, to choose. Will is the initiating power behind all actions and manifestations. Purpose is differentiated will. Suppose a beam of light is projected from your head to the wall; that is your will. Put a section of film between the light and the wall, and you will see a projection of the film onto the wall. That projection is the purpose, will which has differentiated. When you contemplate and figure out how to materialize that projection, you form a plan and use your own will to manifest it on Earth.

The *Great Invocation* eventually aligns your will with the Plan, with the Purpose, and finally with the Will of God. It is at this stage of achievement that you may say:

Thy Will be done.

When new energies are available and new heights in consciousness are reached on all three levels of the personality, many old forms will be discarded, *i.e.* those forms which serve the hatred of people, such as the tools of warfare. Can you imagine what a great release it will be for the human soul once it discards such forms from its personality life? People will be less and less willing to work in factories which produce such destructive products. Other forms that serve crime, that perpetuate the vices of people — not only on the physical plane, but also on the emotional plane — will also be discarded, as well as many forms of obsolete words and expressions. On the mental plane, many thought-forms that serve the vices of man and generate separation, hatred, ignorance, exploitation and crime will be discarded. Those who enter into communication with the Lords of Light, Love and Power can no longer employ thoughtforms that breed separation, crime, destruction and illusion.

For the individual and humanity as a whole, an entirely new environment will be created which will correspond to those changes in consciousness resulting from triangle work. Thus, obsolete forms will be discarded, and new forms will be created to serve the spiritual endeavors of mankind, in order to bring unity, understanding and cooperation to all humanity. These forms will be harmonious with New-Age energies, and expressive of New-Age values.

It is very possible that the human form on three levels will change in order to be able to better transmit and use New-Age visions, communications and expressions. Thus, "Old Age" body-types will be phased out, and new kinds of bodies will be born, better equipped on three levels, with greatly unfolded centers of energy, senses, nervous systems and glands. The race of men will achieve a rare degree of beauty as a result of being in harmony with the prototypical sources of creative energy.

This will also have a great effect on the forms of Nature. As one kingdom advances, it opens the road of progress for others. As a result of such an advance, forms that cannot adapt to higher frequencies of energy die out.

Those who build triangles together create a closer relationship with each other on the mental plane. In the future, such relationships can be used for telepathic communication with each other to enrich each other's lives, to cooperate in great projects, and to stand united with each other in times of world and personal crises. Thus, people who aspire together, people who work together, gradually come closer to each other and form a band of workers for the Plan of the Hierarchy. It is possible that if they are serious in their triangle work, in future incarnations they may form families, or become close associates on the physical plane.

Group members often incarnate in the same area or during the same time period, and attract each other to continue their group service to the world, according to the need of the time.

When you are doing triangle work, you must be positive, loving and willing to do the work. Of course, your heart and mind must be involved in the work, and it is important to do your triangle work with joy and interest. If you do your triangle work in a mechanical way, or while in a negative or depressed mood, it is possible that you may infect others with your condition. That is why it is suggested that before you do your triangle work, you uplift your consciousness above all that is not of real value in the eyes of the Soul, and from the viewpoint of Infinity.

7

Deeper Layers of the Great Invocation

*T*he *Great Invocation*, which was given in 1945, is now translated into one hundred forty languages. Everywhere in the world people are using the *Great Invocation* with wonderful results.

The *Great Invocation* was given to humanity to connect the points of the electrical wires in man, in nations, within the centers of the planet, solar system, Zodiac and galaxy. When used with enthusiasm and fixed determination, the *Great Invocation* eventually brings alignment within all these points; humanity as a whole receives "life more abundant," as referred to by a Great One.

In *A Treatise on Cosmic Fire*, we read:

> . . . When the primordial ray of intelligent activity, the divine ray of intelligent love, and the third cosmic ray of intelligent will meet, blend, merge, and blaze forth, the Logos will take His fifth initiation, thus completing one of His cycles.[1]

---

[1]Bailey, Alice A., p. 45.

The *Great Invocation* is a labor given to humanity to assist in the fulfillment of such an event. If humanity sounds the *Great Invocation* in increasing numbers, then Light, Love and Power will "meet, blend, merge, and blaze forth," not only in man, but also in the planet and in the Universe, thus helping our Logos take the Fifth Initiation, making this planet sacred.

As these three rays "merge and blaze forth," humanity will go through a process of transformation and transfiguration, because humanity is a center in the Body of the Logos Who, in taking the Fifth Initiation, will make His whole Body sacred. This is why sounding the *Great Invocation* is not only a service for individuals, but for humanity — as well as for the Planetary Logos in Whose Body we are living cells.

The Universe is constructed like a spider's web. If we think about and study the energy patterns of the Universe, we will see that it is like a spherical spider's web. The crisscrossing points of this web are called centers, or points. The whole secret of success and power is to connect with these points of intersection. For example, unlinked electrical systems may exist, but they do not have power. As soon as they are fused and hooked up, energy immediately starts circulating. The greater the linkage, the greater the energy. This also applies to the human being.

A person has seven main chakras and seventy-seven chakras total. This system is an unlinked spider's web in the body. Initiation and development, progress and prosperity depend on linkage. For example, if the seventh and first centers are linked, a person radiates will power. If the fourth and second centers are linked, he radiates love. If the third and fifth centers are linked, he radiates light. If all centers are linked, he is a glorious human being.

When you think about the Universe, about the stars and galaxies, think of them as a spider's web of energy. The whole creation, from the smallest insect, to man, to Divine Beings, is trying to link these points together. If a person is able to link these points, he becomes a powerhouse in himself, for the planet, for the solar system, galaxy and Cosmos.

Speaking about the Cosmos, the Tibetan Master says that the whole Cosmos is surrounded by an etheric web on which manifested human beings travel like a spider, linking themselves from one point to another. Earth has its webs. In esoteric understanding, a pilgrimage is a process of connecting one point to another. Those who travel on Earth create a linkage when they go from one point to certain places, making that spider's web alive with their presence and energy. They link centers together.

All of our progress, enlightenment and initiations, are based on linking these centers within ourselves, tying these points together so that eventually our individual webs, the planetary and solar webs and the Cosmic web are all enlightened with our consciousness and with our presence. This is how we become omniscient, omnipotent and omnipresent. Telepathy is based totally upon this principle. For example, if your telephone line is cut, you cannot communicate. But if there is a connecting line, you can communicate.

The line is installed, but we do not know how to use it. The whole web exists. God created the web; God is that intricate web. Through that web, God's Power — Light, Energy, Love — is circulating. Whoever connects with this web and makes contact with the Central Power, the energy fields, is charged to his degree of contact.

One of the causes of greatness is a process of *tuning in*. Let us say that you have a beautiful radio or television, but that you cannot tune into any stations. If you cannot "tune in" to the stations, you are blank. Only when you are tuned in is your whole mechanism in operation. It is just a matter of turning the "dial" a degree one way or the other.

The Great Ones gave prayers, invocations and mantrams to facilitate and make human beings contact this web and eventually manifest the resultant charge through human expression, creativity and service. Prayers, invocations and mantrams are techniques, teachings which help us tune to the web. The *Great Invocation* is one of these. The Tibetan Master, speaking about the *Great Invocation*, says that it is the mantram of Christ. He says that Christ has stood for ages in the Presence of the Hierarchy and intoned it at His specific level.

At His own level, Christ was trying to activate parts of that Cosmic web to bring to humanity the energies of Light, Love and Divine Will. He was trying to activate just a part of that web, because if the entire voltage of the web was released, humanity would go berserk. They could not handle the energy.

Great change and preparation were given to humanity during World War II, which brought to the surface of life a great degree of expansion in consciousness and purification — as well as lots of "dirt," obsession and possession. After this war, the *Great Invocation* was given to humanity so that it could link itself in four dimensions:

1. individually, as human beings linking the webs within themselves;
2. with webs in the planet;
3. with webs in the solar system; and
4. with webs in the galaxy or Cosmos.

How deeply the *Great Invocation* is known, how much control a person has in his visualization and spiritual understanding, how much time and energy he gives when saying the *Great Invocation*, determine how the Universe responds to him. It all depends on his own efforts. The Universe responds to a person with the exact same amount he puts into the Universe.

Many religions, philosophies and so-called "teachings" commit a grave error, the root of all deception and confusion, when they teach that God is "out there" and that we are "here," that the Universe is "out there" and that we are "here." The Ageless Wisdom says that everything exists within the human being; nothing exists outside. To teach otherwise is incorrect. When we talk about ourselves, we are talking about AUM. AUM is within us and we are within AUM.

To explain this further, a person is both a bubble in the ocean — and he is the ocean itself. As a person says the *Great Invocation*, he links three centers within himself which automatically, gradually and eventually link him with three points in the planet, three points in the solar system and three points in the Cosmos. These three points, or centers, are: *the point of Light, the point of Love,* and *the center where the Will of God is known.*

There are three chakras, or three glands within the brain — the pineal, pituitary and carotid glands — which are activated when a person says the *Great Invocation*. The corresponding chakras — the throat, heart and head chakras — are also activated: the throat chakra is intelligence, or Light; the heart chakra is Love; and the head center is Divine Power, or Will.

Through this linkage a person creates a circulation of energy within his system. He cannot activate anything in the Universe unless the corresponding points are activated within himself. Nothing can be activated in the Universe unless the corresponding points within a person are activated. The stars do not have power upon us unless we give them the power to influence; our sacredness is protected. To understand this, we must clean out the trash which has accumulated in our consciousness for thousands of years.

Our health, prosperity, success, power and glory, depend on the degree in which we are able to connect these centers and to what degree we are able to use them in equilibrium, in balance and in the right dosage. By observing what we do or say, we can sometimes catch ourselves by noting, "In the words I spoke, there was Light, but no Love. This is not good. In my action there was Will Power, but no Love. This will not work."

Any creation that is not balanced with these three systems, with these three laws, with these three great rays, is futile. It creates karma, difficulties and obstacles, so that we come back and learn how to unite these three centers. In some books there is Light, but no Love and Purpose. In some books there is Love, but no intellect. In others, there is no Light, energy or Love. When these three are not combined, there is only failure. When they are combined properly, we have physical, emotional, mental, spiritual and divine success.

When the heart is activated, divine compassion is already present as Love. When the throat center is activated, divine, pure knowledge is immediately available; you do not even need to learn. When the head center is activated, Purpose is there. You lead a purposeful life; you do not become a burden on others, leeching off of them or exploiting them. To live a purposeful life means that the individual, the planet, the solar system and the galaxy are all tuned to each other. Such a person does not do anything that is considered wrong within these four dimensions. He is tuned within himself.

Unsuccessful human beings have no linkage. Their centers work independently; there is no linkage between them. The Tibetan Master once said that initiation is observed by the geometrical awakenings of the centers. There is a geometry that must connect the centers — circles, triangles and squares. If a person is connected by squares, he has an old-fashioned, out-moded intellect. If he is triangular, he is striving. If the linkage of the centers is circular, he is a great disciple or Initiate.

We are striving to connect three centers within ourselves. People think they are aligned, at-one and integrated, but they are not. In fact, very few people are. The heart often functions by itself. In this case, the heart is very beautiful, but there is no intelligence and no purpose. We sometimes call these people, *goody-goody*, or *wishy-washy*. They hallucinate. Sometimes the throat center works without heart and purpose. This is evil — pure exploitive intellect that manipulates and "eats the bones" of others, leaving them desperate. Will Power is total destruction if it is not balanced with Light and Love.

The *Great Invocation* is a technique, a discipline we can exercise to link these three centers to make us balanced human beings with Love, Intellect and Will Power. Thought is the "spider." Thinking is to do the work of a spider, to spin and connect. Thinking means to link one point with another. By voicing the thought, *"Let Light descend on Earth,"* a person really charges the action of the "spider" with **fire.** Speech is fire; it is creative. Voice and sound are creative, electrical fire.

The *Great Invocation* was given to teach humanity the ABCs of connecting these three points — Light, Love and Power — within the human psyche, within the planet and the Universe. By connecting these three points, the human psyche later becomes a "radio receiver" for greater and greater stations. This is how the teaching of the *Great Invocation* must be presented to humanity.

We cannot reach a higher center of Light if the corresponding center within us is not activated. Great prophets and persons of great power know how to connect the sources of Power, Light and Beauty, because the corresponding centers are active within themselves.

While saying the *Great Invocation,* visualize three centers within you as you say,*"Let Light and Love and Power restore the Plan on Earth."* What is the Plan? The Plan is the life that you must live and organize in the light of the Divine Plan. Your part of the construction in the great building is your plan. For example, your plan is to paint; that is your part of the Plan. Maybe later you will be an electrician; or being a roofer might be your plan.

When saying the *Great Invocation,* we must first consider that we are trying to connect these three points within ourselves in order to build a mechanism of transformation.

Transformation is the process by which a person creates a radioactive center of Light within himself, so that his whole mental body is slowly illuminated. When we evoke Light and Love, the Love center opens and our whole emotional nature will be enlightened. When we evoke the highest center — Purpose, Will — our body will be transformed. The highest affects the lowest body, and so on. The three centers transform one's being when they are linked together; the person then becomes a triangle, a pyramid, a balanced human being, because he has Light, Love and Power.

When a person builds that pyramid, that triangle, within himself, he can then connect to the three planetary centers. One of these centers is called, *the intelligence of humanity, the Light in humanity*. The second center is called *the Hierarchy*, and the third center is called *Shamballa*. A person is able to draw into himself the wisdom that exists in humanity from individuals and groups in or out of incarnation, with his throat center. All of the great "Intelligences" Who have accumulated wisdom and knowledge throughout ages, can be transmitted through the throat center.

We had a Teacher who never attended or graduated from any school. But he knew the answers to any question. I once asked him how he knew so many things. He replied, "You see this cup? Fill it in the nearby lake and bring it back to me." When I brought the cup back to him, he said, "This cup is now full. But if I create a pump to drain the lake into this cup, my cup will always be full." His throat center was so open that whatever question a person asked, he would simply pause a little, tune in to a center, and draw the answer from it.

A Great Master was once asked, "How do the Masters know all of these things?" He replied, "We don't need to know. We can connect Our 'telephone line' and immediately receive an answer." This is an example of the extension of the human triangle into the Planetary Triangle: Love, Compassion, Wisdom — the Hierarchy. Courage, daring and great works of construction and destruction are a connection through Shamballa, the center where the Will of God is known. In Christian literature, Shamballa is known as, "My Father's House." Christ once said, "There are many mansions in My Father's House."

When a person activates the triangle within himself, he is activating the Planetary Triangle, and becoming an outpost of consciousness for three planetary centers.

There was a man in the monastery who would talk with us from sunset until the following morning and keep us alive. Afterwards, we were not sleepy. In the afternoon we would eat, swim, then sit and talk with him again. He would pour and pour and pour. One day I asked how he was able to do this. "I am one with everything that exists," was his reply. The network of Light, Love and Power was connected within him to a great degree.

When a person connects his **throat center** with the throat center of the planet, he begins to understand the human mystery — human misery, human pain, human striving, human dreams and human visions. From that day on, he will never be a separative, exploitative person. His six vipers — hatred, anger, fear, revenge, jealousy and greed — will evaporate. These are six vipers upon which humanity dances. All war, hatred, division and separation are rooted in these six vipers. Fear creates many events in the world. We sometimes think that these events are righteous, but fear creates them. If we see our wrong-doings, we will find the devil of fear at their roots.

When a person connects his **heart center** with the Hierarchy, the wisdom and inclusiveness of the Hierarchy manifest in his life. He will understand everything; he will love and see everything. And no matter what he sees, whatever he understands, what information he has, he will never act without compassion. This is the main key.

The root of forgiveness and lovingness is connected with this tie to the Hierarchy. When a person has that communication tie, that ability to "tune in," he is a compassionate person.

When a person's **head center** is connected with the head center of the planet, he loses his little will. This is such a paradox. Desire, emotion, greed, fear and jealousy, separatism and antagonism, gossip, slander, treason are not Will. Unless we reach the same conclusion that Christ reached when He said, "Thy Will be done," we will not have real will at all. This is how we can unite with Supreme Will.

At this stage of our evolution, how can we put this into practice? It seems as if we often need lots of suffering to understand. But to make this higher connection easy, the Great Ones gave us the *Great Invocation* so that we could begin to learn how to connect the "spider's web" of the Cosmos. In reciting the *Great Invocation*, we start activating the Solar Triangle, which consists of the Central Spiritual Sun, the heart of the sun, and the sun.

Human intelligence is connected to the sun — literally, the light of the sun — through the throat center. If the sun ceases to shine, there will no longer be light. Our planet would become a moon; our brain would become a moon. My grandmother used to advise me not to make important decisions at night. "Wait until dawn breaks so that the sun rises in back of the mountain and *gives* you a decision," she would say. Her advice proved true. I observed that the decisions I made in darkness brought suffering with them. Life is an experience and experiment for me. By jumping in, making mistakes, doing good and false things alike, I eventually shook myself from all of them, like a bird shakes its feathers, and said, "Now I have learned my lesson."

When a person's heart center is connected with the Hierarchy and with the heart of the sun, he becomes a Zoroaster, a Buddha, a Christ, a Moses. What will happen when the head center is connected with Shamballa and with the center of the Spiritual Sun? Since no one, as yet, has accomplished this, we do not know. We are waiting for such people.

To go beyond, we must connect three greater centers: the Great Bear, the Pleiades and Sirius. The Pleiades is intellect, the Mother aspect, the Holy Spirit aspect, the Shekina aspect. Sirius is the heart. The Great Bear is the House of God in the Cosmos. Four stations exist beyond these, but our current intellect cannot begin to penetrate to this level.

We turn now to a few practical aspects. Of course, the above information is good because it expands our consciousness and makes us realize that when we say the *Great Invocation*, we are not playing; instead we are engaged in very serious and important business.

The *Great Invocation*, simply stated, is used for great achievements. If we want to achieve, to be prosperous, creative and powerful, we must say the *Great Invocation*. **It is the greatest mantram**, with no intention of insulting all other mantrams. The *Great Invocation* is a synthesizer.

In order to begin saying the *Great Invocation* correctly, we must be able to concentrate our mind. Prior to one of my lectures in Washington, D.C., we said the *Great Invocation* together. Afterward, I asked how many people thought of nothing else but the *Great Invocation* while they were saying it. No one raised his hand.

This is not the way to say the *Great Invocation*. When we say the *Great Invocation*, we must be in the *Great Invocation* — nowhere else. A person who learns to do this will advance six hundred incarnations in six months; this is no exaggeration.

We must totally empty ourselves and focus only on the *Great Invocation*. Successfully accomplishing this, we will connect our heart, throat and head centers with the three centers of the planet, then with the three centers of the solar system, and then, perhaps, with the three centers of the Cosmos — if this is what we really want.

This connection can be augmented by saying the *Great Invocation* for integration, alignment, power, fusion and connection. If a person really wants to make a breakthrough, he will say the *Great Invocation* twenty-one times daily.

I had something to overcome in my nature, so I said the *Great Invocation* twenty-one times daily for one month — and conquered that "devil" in me. When water goes through a pipe, it cleans the pipe. When I connected with the energy of the *Great Invocation* which flowed through me, it cleaned things that were not good. Are there other things to be cleaned within us? Of course! There are millions of things, but we must attack the enemies one by one.

If a person wants to make a breakthrough in his health, he can say the *Great Invocation* twenty-one times daily. For example, when my son was seven, he caught meningitis; he was stiff like a board. When we took him to the hospital, the doctor told us that even if the boy recovered, his eyes, ears, lungs, and so on, would be defective. On the tenth day of his hospitalization, the nurse called to say that he might die that day. I called the family together and said, "Let us say the *Great Invocation*." We visualized him, and poured the energy of Light, Love and Power over him. Two days later the nurse called, saying, "Your son is improving. A miracle is happening." He recovered fully, with no side effects from the illness, and is now a judge.

The *Great Invocation* can be used for healing, for achievement, for enlightenment, for making decisions. When we receive Light, we can make better decisions.

I once decided to take a gun and shoot someone. Then I said, "First let me say the *Great Invocation*; then I will shoot him." After saying the *Great Invocation*, something said, "Put the gun back. Love that man, and say the *Great Invocation* one more time." "Okay," I said. "I'm sorry. I feel very badly about wanting to harm him. Now I have reversed myself."

The *Great Invocation* reveals what to do. It is a very powerful mantram for enlightenment, for increasing our love, for establishing good relations with our friends, husbands, wives and children. I know a family in which the children were going berserk. The father and mother were scattered; the children were abandoned. One day they visited me on my birthday. The father said, "We didn't have a chance to buy you a gift." I said, "You can give me a gift by promising something. Can you collect your family together every morning and say the *Great Invocation* as my gift?" The man said, "You are kidding. What kind of gift is that? You aren't receiving anything!" "Later I will tell you what I received," I assured him. They did it, and one month later the family was united; they loved and respected each other. Something changed them totally. When the father finally asked what I had gained, I told him, "The pleasure of the absence of your quarrels!"

The *Great Invocation* is a mantram. The sounding of a mantram has its own rules, and those who follow those rules receive the benefits of the mantram.

1. The first rule is to say the *Great Invocation* with concentration. Concentration keeps your mind from wandering onto other subjects while sounding the *Great Invocation*. You think only of the words and sentences you are sounding and your mind is clear of any other interference.

This will not be easy. Sometimes your concentration will not last more than a few words or sentences, while your mouth continues to sound the words and sentences mechanically. With effort, you will gradually be able to increase the duration of your concentration.

Often mechanical repetition also has good effects, but these effects cannot be compared to the effects harnessed through concentrated, conscious repetition of the mantram. Whenever the concentration level fails, the mechanical level increases; and when the mechanical level increases, it eventually creates repulsion in the object.

2. The second rule is visualization in concentration. Your concentration should be aimed toward a vision which is kept in your mind through visualization.

What is the vision of the *Great Invocation*? The vision, simply stated, is **God** — the Infinite Presence in the Universe, or Infinity Itself — in which there are three major centers:

the Center of Light;
the Center of Love; and
the Center of Power.

Then there is the Center which is called humanity.

In the first stanza, you concentrate on a *point of Light* and visualize light shining forth into the minds of men, spreading all over the world.

In the second stanza, you visualize Infinity and a *point of Love,* with love spreading forth into the hearts of men.

In the third stanza, you visualize the Almighty Presence and a *point of Power,* from which power is spread as His Will.

Then, *in the fourth stanza,* you visualize humanity, in which Light, Love and Divine Will are creating three conditions in which evil will not have a chance to operate.

In the fifth stanza, you visualize the globe or the world, which is in the process of transformation through these three energies of Light, Love and Power coming from God, from the Almighty Presence.

3.   The third rule is to try to be a source of Light, Love and Divine Will individually in our daily lives, in all our relationships. Unless we concentrate, visualize and try to live the *Great Invocation* in our daily lives, we cannot derive full benefit from it. Full benefit emerges when our lives become centers of Light, Love and Divine Will, and we become evocative to the corresponding energies of the Universe.

Of course, sounding the *Great Invocation* will echo in the Higher Worlds and evoke beneficent energies, which will help humanity find its direction in the midst of present confusion.

A daily practice of concentration not only brings blessings to mankind, but also to our personal lives. As the focus of our concentration and visualization increases, we will notice ourselves becoming more efficient in our office, home and other daily activities, and correspondingly, more successful in life.

The effect of the *Great Invocation* becomes more potent when it is sounded in triangular formation.

There are five essentials to remember when sounding the *Great Invocation* in group formation:

1. *Speak rhythmically and slowly*. Rhythm is essential for the transmission of sound and thought. Rhythm creates momentum in the currents directed toward higher forces or higher centers.

2. *Sound it with deep concentration on the meaning*. This means to realize the meaning of each word you utter. This also means not to let your mind wander to memories, dreams or problems. Any time your thoughts wander, you create disturbances in the mental rhythm of the flow of the *Great Invocation*. The flow or current is sustained by the energy of the concentrated thought.

3. *Sound it with visualization*. You must visualize Light descending on Earth, Love descending into the hearts of men, Christ returning to Earth, and so on. Visualization transmits energy from Higher Sources and keeps your mind on the right track. Visualization also clears away hindrances found on lower levels, and makes the vision actualize.

4.   *When saying the Invocation in group formation, all voices must be blended into one voice.* Sometimes we hear one or two strong voices which try to impose themselves upon all the others. When this happens, people's concentration is disturbed and they are forced to hear the imposed voice(s) rather than following the meaning and significance of the words. In drawing the attention of others to himself, a person makes his ego swell out of proportion. Such a person brings the attention of the group to himself, creating a strong pressure on his aura, which hurts his etheric centers and related organs.

People think that God has weak ears and that one must shout to be heard. The fact is that the most powerful currents of voice are those which are uttered in a whisper. A loud voice is physical and emotional, originating from the solar plexus. A whisper comes from the throat, ajna and head centers and is charged with aspiration and spiritual energies.

5.   *After each stanza, one must pause for three, then seven, then nine, and finally twelve counts.* Each pause must be used for contemplation and visualization in regard to the previous stanza.

When each stanza is backed with a powerful current of thought, it makes the stanza more effective and fruitful. Also, esoterically it gives our auras a chance to charge themselves and fuse with the aura of the group.

During prayer it is important to keep our voices low, even in a state of whispering. We know that in many mystery schools, secrets and passwords are given in a whisper. In Masonic orders, Rosicrucian organizations, and Sufi mysteries, the most important instructions are given in a whisper, because a whisper protects the current and then impresses it upon the mind of the initiate.

Again, the names of Higher Powers are not proclaimed in a loud voice, but are whispered or signalled — for highest respect, for the protection of unready people, and for serious contemplation of the power of the name. The same thing is true when we say something very sacred or secret to each other. Even when we say, "I love you," we do not jump to the highest pitch of our voice. When you are deeply in prayer, you close your doors and whisper to God, or you even talk in your thoughts and heart.

In a whisper, there is concentration and focus. In a whisper, you do not color your voice with your vanities and personal feelings, but you release that which is most essential, with strength and strong frequency. If you are praying or talking to your Soul, know that Its ears can hear you before you even pronounce the words.

In group prayer or invocation, there are three successive stages of potency:

1. you hear only your own voice;
2. you hear the voice of the group as one voice; and
3. you sound the prayer in thought.

A heavy voice disturbs the aura of the owner and his energy follows the line of sound, then the line of thought. Sound does not travel far if it does not have thought. It disperses after radiating a few colors toward the astral plane. If there is thought, then sound turns into color and penetrates into the mental plane. A heavy, strong voice is its own blockage. A whisper or soft voice travels a long distance.

We suggest that in addition to our daily responsibility of sounding the *Great Invocation*, we also sound the following reflective prayer and meditation:

> *My Lord,*
> *let Your fire purify our minds*
> *and cleanse any ugly or dark thoughts*
> *existing in our minds.*

Pause and visualize how the fire of God is cleansing and purifying our minds and the minds of humanity.

> *My Lord,*
> *let Your fire purify our hearts*
> *and burn out all feelings*
> *that are negative, painful and separative.*

Pause again and visualize how the fire of Space is purifying our etheric hearts.

> *My Lord,*
> *restore Your light in our hearts.*
> *Give us courage,*
> *and let Your light shine through*
> *all our thoughts, words, actions,*
> *and fill all our being with joy and bliss,*
> *so that we radiate Your Presence.*

Here again, pause and visualize receiving courage, shining His light and filling ourselves with joy and bliss.

OM   OM   OM   OM   OM

For the first six months, this prayer should be intoned in a whisper. During the next six months, say it in your thoughts so that you start developing the voice of your thoughts. Also, the OMs must be whispered the first six months, and silently intoned during the second six months. Visualize the note and sound it in silence, and also visualize how OM radiates as a light throughout your aura. A silent OM is more powerful; it travels faster and carries more of you than your voice.

In sounding the OM out loud, you are limited to the air in your lungs. A silent OM can be sustained for any length of time you want, without diffusing your concentration. Beginners need the help of color, word and voice; but disciples learn to surpass these aids, because they can concentrate without these aids.

If the OM is silently sounded in a focused and concentrated way in which there are no disturbances, you can sound it for a few minutes, charging your sound with great energy and meaning through your visualization. Visualization is more successful in silence.

Some people exaggerate in sounding the OM. There is great danger here. One must go slowly so that his aura gets used to the vibration and the transformative process of the OM. If you go slowly, you can make your aura absorb the energy of the OM and slowly transform and transmute its atoms without creating disturbances in the aura. If you hurry and force your aura in exaggeration, you may nourish in it the seeds of weeds; and before you know it, weeds will grow and mislead you on the Path by stimulating your various weaker centers and vices.

Transformation must occur on a gradient scale. We have seen people who hurry in zeal and spiritual greed. They are those who fall on the Path, or become the enemies of the Teaching. It is better to become a good gardener and know how to cultivate the lower nature so that it turns into a beautiful garden — one that produces a crop instead of weeds. This garden is the aura, which represents the physical, emotional and mental bodies.

8

Higher Triangles

*I*n one of His writings, Master Djwhal Khul says:

> [C]onstruct a network of light and service in every land [as preparation for the Coming One]. This is begun in the individual environment of the server, and gradually extended throughout the world. It was with this idea in view that I suggested the forming of triangles of people, pledged to use the Invocation and to extend its use through the world. It is my specific plan to help *mass* world thought and thus evoke the Avatar, and likewise to provide a world group through which the new forces and energies can function, the new ideas can spread, and the coming world order find adherents.[1]

The axis of triangle work is the Christ and His future reappearance among men. This is mentioned in esoteric literature as the *third great approach*.

---

[1] Bailey, Alice A., *The Externalisation of the Hierarchy*, p. 312.

Buddhas of Activity.

There is a class of Great Beings called *Buddhas of Activity*, Who cooperate with Sanat Kumara. They form a triad, at the center of which Sanat Kumara stands. In speaking about Them, Master Djwhal Khul says:

> *The mystery of electricity* has three keys, each of which is held in the hands of one of the Buddhas of Activity. Theirs is the prerogative to control the electrical forces of the physical plane, and Theirs the right to direct the three major streams of this type of force in connection with *our present globe*. These three streams are concerned with atomic substance, out of which all forms are constructed.[2]

We are further told that:

> In connection with *our chain* there are three mysterious Entities (of whom our three Pratyeka Buddhas are but the Earth reflections) Who perform a similar function in connection with the electrical forces of the chain. *In the scheme*, the planetary Logos has also three co-operating Existences Who are the summation of His third Aspect, and who perform therefore work similar to that performed by the three aspects of Brahma in the solar system. The mystery of this threefold type of electricity is largely connected with the lesser Builders, with the elemental essence in one

---

[2]Bailey, Alice A., *A Treatise on Cosmic Fire*, p. 873.

particular aspect, — its lowest and most profound for men to apprehend as it concerns the secret of that which "substands" or "stands back" of all that is objective. In a secondary sense it concerns the forces in the ethers which are those which energise and produce the activities of all atoms. Another type deals with the electrical phenomenon which finds its expression in the light which man has somewhat harnessed, in the phenomena such as thunder storms and the manifestation of lightning, with the aurora borealis, and in the production of earthquakes and all volcanic action. All these manifestations are based on electrical activity of some kind, and have to do with the "soul of things," or with the essence of matter.[3]

In the same book, He says:

The Buddhas of Activity, are the Triad Who stands closest to Sanat Kumara, The Lord of the World. They are the planetary correspondences to the three Aspects of the logoic third Aspect and are concerned with the force behind planetary manifestation.[4]

The Logoic Third Aspect is the Ray of Active Intelligence, or the Third Ray. The Second Aspect is the Ray of Love-Wisdom, or Second Ray. The First Aspect is the Ray of Will or Power, the First Ray, or positive energy.

---

[3]*Ibid.*

[4]*Ibid.*, p. 75 (see footnote 32).

The devas are the agents of the divine will because they are a consequence of the point of attainment of our planetary Logos as He exists outside the seven planes of our sphere of existence, the cosmic physical plane. They are conditioned by His cosmic astral and mental vehicles. In a definite sense, they *are* the agents of the Universal Mind, even though they are *not* mental *as we understand that term*. They are sometimes regarded as blind forces, but that is only because they get their inspiration from levels of divine awareness outside the range of the human consciousness, no matter how high, or when used in its widest connotation.

Their controlling Agent in manifestation is the Triangle of Energy to which we give the name the "Three Buddhas of Activity." They are therefore closely connected with the third aspect of divinity. They are essentially the "eye within the Triangle" — a most familiar symbol to many today. They are the expression, in activity, of the "All-Seeing Eye"; through their agency God *sees*, and through them and the energy directed through them, He directs the creative process. They are under the complete control of the three Buddhas of Activity, Who are the cosmic Prototypes of the Lords of the three major rays, but not in the sense usually understood when the rays are considered in their relation to man. They are the correspondence of these three rays and are responsible for the entire manifested universe, but only within the orbit of the third aspect, the expression of the Universal Mind.[5]

. . .The three Buddhas of Activity (Who are also Members of the Great Council) are expressions of the counterparts on cosmic levels of the energies latent in the three permanent atoms in the three worlds of human endeavour. This is again a dangerous parallel to propose for — as a symbol — it lacks any true analogy.[6]

Group discipleship, group initiation, is the characteristic of the New Age. When through meditation, service and striving, a group of people build their own rainbow bridges, these lines of communication eventually blend and fuse with each other, forming one completed Antahkarana with three distinct strands — the life thread, the consciousness thread and the creative thread.

This rainbow extends from the head, ajna and alta major centers of the Initiate toward the three points of the Spiritual Triad, anchoring itself in the three points of the Council Chamber of Shamballa. These three points are called the three Buddhas of Activity.

Thus, the consciousness and awareness of the Initiate extend not only to the Spiritual Triad, radiating will, love and pure intelligence, but they also penetrate the sphere of Shamballa and become impressed with the Purpose of the Planetary Logos. In other words, the brain of the Initiate and

---

[5]Bailey, Alice A., *The Rays and The Initiations*, pp. 179-180.
[6]*Ibid.*, p. 206.

the planetary brain make contact. Through such an alignment, great revelations will manifest on Earth.

Master Djwhal Khul says:

> . . . The words "Higher Three" refer to the three Buddhas of Activity Who still remain actively cooperating with the Lord of the World. . . . They do not belong to this solar system at all; They have passed through the human stage in such far distant and remote world cycles that the experience is no longer a part of Their consciousness; They act as advisors to Sanat Kumara where His initial purpose is concerned. . . . It is Their supreme task to see that, in the Council Chamber of Shamballa, that purpose is ever held steadily within the "area of preparation" . . . of that Council. They function, in a peculiar sense, as linking intermediaries between the Logos of our solar system and the informing Life of the constellation Libra; They relate these two great centres of energy to our planetary Logos.

> In the last solar system They were the planetary Logoi of three planets in which the mind principle reached its highest stage of development; They embody in Themselves . . . the wisdom aspect of the second ray, as it . . . has been called in the Bhagavad Gita "skill in action." Hence Their name, the Buddhas of Activity.

> Sanat Kumara has now moved one step ahead of Them upon the great cosmic ladder

of evolution, for an aspect of the Law of Sacrifice has conditioned Them. However, within the planetary consciousness and among Those Who work out the divine purposes, there are none Who approach the Eternal Youth and these three Buddhas in point of Evolution. They work . . . through the medium of the Lords of the Seven Rays. . . . They are to Sanat Kumara what the three mind aspects upon the mental plane are to the disciple and the initiate. They represent in action:

> The concrete or lower mind of the planetary Logos,
>
> That energy which we call the soul and which the disciple calls "the Son of Mind,"
>
> The higher or abstract mind,

but all this from cosmic levels and with cosmic implications. It was Their activity which . . . brought about the act of individualisation and thus brought the human kingdom into existence. . . . [T]he three Buddhas of Activity are responsible for:

1. *The Act of Individualisation.* The work of the particular Buddha responsible at the time for this major activity, has been temporarily quiescent since Lemurian days. He works, when active, through the seventh ray and draws the needed energy from two constellations: Cancer and Gemini.

2. *The Act of Initiation.* I would call your attention to the word *act*; I am not here referring to process. His work only begins at the third initiation when the planetary Logos is the Initiator. At that initiation, the will aspect begins to function. The Buddha behind the initiatory process is extremely active at this time; He works through the Christ and the Lord of the second ray, drawing the needed energy from the constellations Capricorn and Aquarius.

3. *The Act of Identification.* This involves what has been called a "moment of opening-up," during which the initiate sees that which lies within the cosmic intent and begins to function not only as a planetary unit but as a cosmic focal point. The Buddha of Activity, responsible for this type of planetary activity, works with the Lord of the first ray and functions as an outpost of the consciousness of the informing life of Aries and of Leo. His work is only now beginning to assume importance.[7]

Master Djwhal Khul indicates five triangles:

1. [T]he three Buddhas of Activity Who create a triangle, closely related to the planet Saturn.

2. The triangle of the three rays through whom the three Buddhas work.

[7]*Ibid.*, pp. 267-269.

3.   The three planets which are connected with the three Lords of the three rays and by means of which They express Their impelling energy.

4-5. Two interlaced triangles, created by the six constellations from which the three Buddhas of Activity draw Their needed energy and to which They are uniquely related through Their individual karma. . . .

From the Law of Analogy, another exceedingly important triangle is found in the human body and (esoterically considered) is related to the subject under consideration:

1.   *The ajna centre*, embodying the directing energy of that body of activity which we call the personality.

2.   *The throat centre*, which . . . has a small symbolic triangle of its own, to which I would call attention: the thyroid gland and the parathyroids.

3.   *The centre at the base of the spine.* This is galvanised into activity at a certain stage of the evolutionary process, by energy emanating from the Buddhas of Activity Who are the least active at this particular time. It is an energy pouring towards the fourth kingdom but *not* directed towards any individual. These great Lives work through major groups. . . .[8]

---

[8]*Ibid.*, pp. 269-270.

All of this information has been given here to prepare our minds, so that we can understand the tremendous importance of the following words of Master Djwhal Khul:

> . . . As humanity builds or creates the triangles of light and of goodwill, they are in reality invoking a response activity from two of the Buddhas of Activity — the One Who works through the medium of the will aspect, and the One Who works through love in humanity, *intelligently* applied. . . . The Buddhas Themselves form a deeply esoteric Triangle.

> The two types of triangles now being created by a mere handful of people [referring to 1946-1947] are related to that basic triangle. A third type of triangle will at some much later date be constructed but only when these two earlier types are well established in the consciousness of humanity. Then the activity of all the three Buddhas will be involved and present, and a major planetary integration will take place. . . .

> The triangles of light and of goodwill are essentially invocative. . . . Their strength is dependent upon the depth of feeling in the one case, and the strength of the will in the other, with which they are created. . . . This work *must* go on.[9]

---

[9]*Ibid.*, pp 273-274.

There is also some very interesting information about Divine Messengers. According to the Ageless Wisdom, there are nine classes of these Messengers, which are "three classes of triadic transmitters."

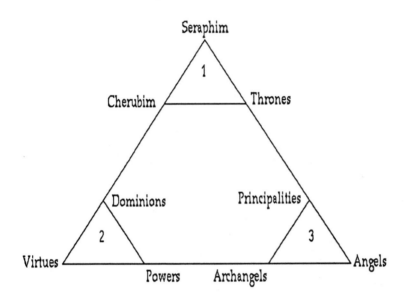

First Triad: Seraphim
                      Cherubim
                      Thrones

Second Triad: Dominions
                      Virtues
                      Powers

Third Triad: Principalities
                      Archangels
                      Angels

Each triad forms three separate triangles which together constitute one triangle as a whole. Below angels are men. Above the Seraphim is the One.

9

Individual Use of the Great Invocation

*T*he *Great Invocation* is essentially a prayer which synthesizes the highest desire, aspiration and spiritual demand of the very soul of humanity.

No one can use this Invocation or prayer for illumination and for love without causing powerful changes in his own attitudes; his life intention, character and goals will be changed and his life will be altered and made spiritually useful.[1]

In New York in 1945, at the time of the June full moon, the *Great Invocation* was given to us. It has become a world invocation or prayer over these last four decades, and has been translated into more than one hundred forty languages; it is broadcasted every day over many radio stations, and is used in churches and brotherhoods in nearly all countries. Thousands of people have written about this wonderful Invocation. It has also been made available to the deaf and the blind.

---

[1]Bailey, Alice A., *Discipleship in the New Age*, Vol. II, p. 168.

People have expressed a sincere acceptance of the Invocation because: a) it contains an urgent message to all humanity; b) the human heart is sensitive to sublime beauties; and c) the world is in need of true guidance and leadership.

Throughout the centuries, many forms of prayer, ritual and invocation have been given to humanity. They have enflamed the emotions and thoughts of mankind, and have led us toward horizons of true survival, toward higher visions of divine achievement. In a sense, they have formed a blueprint to be constructed, a goal to be attained, a task to be fulfilled.

First of all, prayer and invocation attract the aspiration, vision and hope of the best minds of the race. Secondly, they penetrate into the mind and heart of the masses, creating new response, awakening and determination. Thus, mankind slowly advances higher and higher upon the path of unfoldment.

As an example, let us take an invocation which was given to us in a different era:

> *O Thou Who givest sustenance to the Universe,*
> *From Whom all things proceed,*
> *To Whom all things return,*
> *Unveil to us the face of the true spiritual Sun,*
> *Hidden in a disc of golden light,*
> *That we may know the truth*
> *And do our whole duty*
> *As we journey to Thy Sacred Feet.*

We can imagine how great the effect of this invocation was on the people who used it in their meditation and vocal aspirations. It is probable that those who used it sincerely created in themselves a new way of thinking, feeling and acting. It directed their eyes toward That to Which everything returns.

The culture of mankind is the materialized form of all those great aspirations which have been expressed in the human heart and soul throughout centuries, which produced new civilizations and eras. In ancient times, these aspirations and urges were given to humanity by wise men who knew how to direct human emotion and thought through rhythmic prayer, invocation, solemn pledge, and through parables and proverbs.

Prayer and invocation have two degrees of influence. In the first degree, invocation and prayer have a suggestive influence. It may be group self-suggestion in which the person who uses it releases in himself a new urge toward a better life, which surpasses his former self or state of being. In the second degree, it is pure invocation which is directed toward a Great Power about Whom there is no doubt in the user's mind.

Consider the first case. When an invocation or prayer is repeated daily, year after year, with attention and meditation, it produces a real change in man toward betterment. If we recite a prayer or an invocation and meditate upon it, it creates a rhythm in our mental and emotional processes. This rhythmic influence gradually becomes stronger, and changes our way of living and acting. That is why we so often repeat our national songs or anthems, vows, different pledges and mottos. They really affect us and create in us a uniform orientation toward the goal of the invocation.

How much greater is the influence of a pledge or invocation if behind it there are enthusiasm and the recognition of a goal to be achieved. When we truly have faith in the goal expressed in the invocation, when we are able to see the beauty that could be ours by working toward that goal, the rest becomes easy, because sooner or later, strong determination is created in us to achieve that goal in the course of our life.

In the second case, we not only have faith in the goal expressed through the invocation, but we also have faith in that which exists as the Source of creation. When sounding an invocation, we direct our whole being toward that great Existence, evoking response from Him. We direct our "radar" toward Space, and receive from Space rays enriched with a new response. We contact a higher level of consciousness, a new source of inspiration and energy.

Throughout the ages, the dimensions of prayer have gradually shifted to higher levels. In the early ages, masses prayed for the fulfillment of physical and emotional needs. Prayer then became expressed aspiration for individual enlightenment and love, and a request to be led in the right direction. Prayer then emerged from personal limitation, and became prayer for the family, group, nation, and eventually for all humanity. Thus, to the degree that the purpose of prayer changed, the wording of prayer also changed — and in relation to these changes, the level and the target of prayer also changed.

In past centuries, we asked; we demanded. But in the New Age, we will direct higher energies into the fields of human endeavor. We know that Space is an ocean of energy waves in which numerous currents meet, strengthen each other, and transmute or control one another. Mystics of the past used to say that the spark-light produced by a glow-worm would exist for eons, floating and expanding in Space. They also said that just like the subtler light of the glow-worm, every vocal expression continued its existence in Space, in some way.

We know that nothing in the Universe is lost; it is only transformed, transmuted into a different form and expressed again in a different way. If not a single atom is lost, this means that not a single wave of energy is lost. If this is true, then none of our emotional or mental waves are lost; and if they are not lost, they continue their good or bad effects upon human conduct and life.

> *A pure thought ever ascends.*
> *At the feet of Christ it blossoms, radiant.*
> *With pure blue flame glows the Calling Word and*
> *   radiates the Chalice of Exaltation.*
> *O Lord, drain our tears and perceive the flame of*
> *   our heart.*
> *"By flames shall I dry thy tears and upraise the*
> *   temple of thy heart."*[2]

When we depart from our loved ones, we use expressions of goodwill, such as, "Have a nice trip," "God be with you," "We wish you success," and so on. With such words, we impart a protective aura or a wave of inspiration and source of sincere joy to them. It is for the same reason that many parents pray for their children and family members to be spared from any danger or temptation, that they live in the light of their highest dreams and visions. Many people pray every morning and night for their loved ones and for

---

[2]Agni Yoga Society, *Leaves of Morya's Garden*, Vol. I, para. 21.

humanity as a whole, thus projecting into Space a purifying wave of energy — a blessing.

The effect of prayer does not stop here; it is an expanding incense, an illuminating agent, a beam of energy directed toward the Central Power, serving as a channel to that Power. There is an appeal and an answer — invocation and evocation.

When the need is clearly defined, when the fiery aspiration to meet that need is kindled in the heart of the invoking one, then the answer is certain and timely. But to Whom do we appeal? He is the One in Whom we "live, move and have our being." He is the Great Presence, the All-Penetrating Presence.

We live under the illusion that it is only man who is conscious. But man is just an atom, compared to planetary existence. How much smaller he appears if we compare him to a solar system, or to the whole Cosmos. If such an insignificant atom has its own consciousness, isn't it logical to think that atoms smaller than we have consciousness, and conversely, that something larger than we, such as a planet or solar system, has consciousness with which it controls its physical body — a body that is born, lives, grows and one day dies, just as the human body does? This consciousness guides the activity of that huge body, supporting it and using it in the great Cosmic Plan, just as the human soul uses the human body.

Every cell in our body has its own individual life and consciousness. Collectively, it has body-life and body-consciousness. Isn't this the same relationship which exists between the planet, the solar system, and the individual — who is just an atom or cell when compared to the planet or solar system? If this is true, we can say that there is a Presence Who is everywhere and in everything, in which everything lives, moves and breathes.

In certain holy sanctuaries, there is a large eye painted above the altar. This is a wonderful symbol, expressing the omnipresence of the Great Existence. But Who is He? The greatest minds in humanity tell us that He is Life. He is the Consciousness which supports and nourishes all and everything.

They also say that everything is Life; everything is materialized, crystallized Life, that Life is everywhere — from the atom to limitless Space. Space itself is Life, an ocean of Life — electricity — and this Great Life involves everything.

Throughout the ages, wise ones have told us that this Great Life has three aspects which are present in every atom and cell. Although they are sometimes imprisoned, they are ever-ready to be released. There is no lifeless matter or lifeless object. Everything is a part of the Great Life, and it is Life. Everything emerges from that One Life, and returns to the same Life.

We are told that the whole creation is like a figure eight (8). Creation starts from a formless "circle," and begins to materialize through the mid-point, toward the lower "circle," then gradually rises again toward the formless circle.

The *Bhagavad Gita* expresses this idea very beautifully:

> *All beings were in a state of unmanifestation at their beginning. At the mid-course, they came into manifestation. At the end, they will*

again enter into the unmanifested state. Then why grieve?[3]

Life flows through this great figure eight like an electrical current, materializing and dematerializing continuously — but remaining as a whole.

We are also told that He is Light, Love and Will. In other words, He is the Creative Power, the Consciousness of Unity, the Essence of the One Law from Whom radiate all Cosmic, universal, planetary and social laws in their pure differentiations. He is creativity; He is awareness; He is the Law in every form and in every phenomenon.

Christians say that He is the Father, the Son and the Holy Spirit — and also one God. There are also people who define Him as positive Cosmic electricity — the negative electricity and light which emerge when they contact each other.

We are told that this Three-In-One Energy has Its own individual foci, stations and centers through which It expresses Itself and acts, fulfilling the Will of the Central Life. Each aspect of the Three-In-One Energy has its own centers in extra-planetary, inter-planetary, planetary, human and atomic fields, through which it flows, keeping the whole creation alive in a single Will.

The *Great Invocation* invokes these three energies through all kingdoms of Nature, toward extra-systemic fields where they are centralized with their all-pervading presence. It is the first time in the history of humanity that:

a. these three centers are invoked simultaneously by humanity;

---

[3]Translated by H. (Torkom) Saraydarian, Chapter 2, Verse 28.

b. the energies required to meet the planetary needs are so clearly identified; and

c. all methods are used to make the *Great Invocation* the only aspiration of humanity, everywhere and in every race, "[t]o focus the inchoate mass demand of humanity on to the highest possible level."[4]

How to Recite the Invocation.

When we repeat a prayer or invocation, we have a tendency to become mechanical after a while. We utter the words and sentences without conscious participation, and reap no results.

At the time we say the *Great Invocation,* we must proceed through the following steps:

1. a moment of mental silence;
2. a state of penetrative concentration on the meanings of the words; and
3. the use of creative visualization.

Mental silence means detachment from former or new thoughts. *Concentration* is to focus on each word without letting the mind waver, penetrating into the deeper meanings of each word. *Creative visualization* is a process of handling energy and building communication lines to higher levels of being.

All the words that we speak are charged with energy from various levels of our being. If our utterance is mechanical, the words have little power. If we are emotional, they have more power. When we penetrate into the true meaning

[4]Bailey, Alice A., *Discipleship in the New Age*, Vol. II, p. 188.

of our words, they are charged with still more energy. If our consciousness, or being, is focused on higher planes while we speak, our words carry tremendous energy with them, spreading creative effects into Space for a very long time.

When we sound an invocation with concentration, visualization and right tonality, we create a magnetic symphony of colors in Space. The Great Law responds with Power, Love, Light and Beauty. Thus, our needs are fulfilled.

When the *Great Invocation* is intoned by an enlightened group, we have at our disposal the greatest tool to control and handle divine energies in Nature. The *Great Invocation* is a mantram, a word of power.

When we climb the first peak of our being and enter into communication with our Inner Guide, we will sound the Invocation with clear attention, with fiery aspiration and with creative visualization. Mantrams or invocations are more effective when they are sounded from the highest mental levels. This takes preparation, alignment and Soul-infusion. This is the first music that a Soul-infused personality plays or sounds; through it the lower vehicles are charged with great energies of Light, Love and Power. Actually, the sounding of the Invocation is an act of extending this alignment toward centers of Light, Love and Power.

Esotericists assume that there are three great Lords Who represent these three centers of energy. They form a triangle, at the center of which Christ stands. These three Lords are:

1. the Avatar of Synthesis, a Cosmic Being Who represents the center of Power;

2. the Spirit of Peace, Who represents the center of Love; and

3. Lord Buddha, Who represents the center of Light.

When we sound this holy mantram, we invoke these three great Lords from Whom Light, Love and Power stream forth. We can use our visualization to deepen our alignment with these three great centers, and evoke the needed energies to "restore the Plan on Earth."

Let us say that we have achieved one-pointed focus; alignment is complete between the soul and its vehicles.

As we repeat the first stanza of the *Great Invocation*, we now use our visualization to see Light descending and spreading Itself in response to our invocation; we see It clearing away the illusions and darkness found within humanity and within the Universe. What great changes occur in our social, economic and political fields, as this Light descends and spreads Itself!

With the next stanza, we visualize the Heart of God, the great Lord of Love — Christ. What vast preparation He is undergoing to reappear on Earth! See how the energy of Love streams forth into the hearts of men, creating fundamental changes within humanity as a whole, establishing right human relations all over the planet. See how Love melts away mountains of hatred, mountains of war machinery and exploitation, all over the world. See how people of the world are becoming really human, and that the New Age of Brotherhood is on its way.

In reciting the third stanza, see how the Purpose of God guides the little wills of men, creating a new world in which humanity consciously explores the mysteries of initiation, and becomes a co-worker of the Purpose.

In the fourth stanza, visualize humanity as a single center in which the Plan of the Hierarchy is working to "seal the door where evil dwells": evils of hatred, separatism, totalitarianism, materialism, war and ignorance.

In the final stanza, extend your vision and invoke Light, Love and Power, without creating specific, limited thoughtforms. Visualization should be general, not particular, as we do not really know what kind of world it is that we will have. If we create details and particular thoughtforms according to our personal levels of sensitivity and understanding, we may unknowingly create obstacles to the manifestation of the Plan.

Sounding the Invocation.

It is sometimes effective to imagine that a Higher Being or great Initiate is sounding the *Great Invocation*, and then repeat it after Him, stanza by stanza.

To make it more potent, listen to the whole stanza, and then repeat it in one breath, without haste. Pause for three counts after the first stanza, seven counts after the second stanza, nine counts after the third stanza, and twelve counts after the fourth stanza. During these periods of silence, concentrate and visualize the effect of the sounded stanza.

The effect of our speech, or invocation, depends upon the level from which we speak or sound it. If a person's consciousness is focused on the physical level only, the vocal effect of his invocation will be relatively weak, and will not create any permanent results. If he is focused on the emotional plane, his invocation or speech carries more force, and creates greater results. If he is focused on the mental plane, then his invocation will be stronger still, having more force and evoking higher responses.

If his focus is on the higher mental plane or the Intuitional Plane, he is a white magician. His invocation and speech are charged with intense, high-voltage energy. He is very creative, in line with the Plan. That is why alignment is so necessary. If alignment is properly done and the consciousness is lifted to the higher mental plane, then the pilgrim has more energy at his command, and his invocation can reach the greater centers, bringing in Light, Love and Power for the upliftment of humanity and for the fulfillment of the Plan.

It is of great help to reflect on each sentence and stanza of the *Great Invocation* in our leisure time. This deepens our understanding of its esoteric meaning. Words spoken or sounded with understanding create greater effects, and extend our focus of consciousness into the higher planes of our being.

10

Understanding the Great Invocation

*W*e can feel the strength of the first stanza of the *Great Invocation* and the need for this appeal when we observe with clear vision the condition of the world, and see — in spite of the increasing Light — the darkness in which we live, move and breathe.

Stanza One.

> *From the point of Light within the*
> *Mind of God*
> *Let light stream forth into the*
> *minds of men.*
> *Let Light descend on Earth.*

These lines evoke the Light within the Mind of God — the Mind which exists in every atom, in every living creature, in every man, in the whole Universe, and in the greater Cosmos — so that the light of reality, the light of meaning, the light of value and righteousness, the light of understanding, may descend into the darkness of human relations and release the beautiful light in every form, revealing the greater Light until day is with us.

It is Light which will dispel darkness from our minds, words, behavior and activities. For the first time, the minds of men will be liberated through new understanding, in a new day's dawn. People will see each other as brothers and sisters, as Sons and Daughters of Light, fused in the Mind of God from Which come all gifts and paths toward the beauty of greater achievement.

It is Light which, on a planetary scale, will burn and dispel lies, hatred and hypocrisy, all of which are based upon our common selfish urges and interests. It is Light which will show us the meaning of Life, the higher calling, the Plan, the destination toward which we are traveling. It enables us to live a life of light on the path of Light.

A Sufi mystic once said, "If you open the heart of any stone, you will find a radiating sun." It is this sun which is invoked — through all atoms, human beings and universes. What a great vision will open in our souls if we use our creative imagination to visualize a coming civilization, one created by such Light that the human mind is aligned with the Mind of God, acting as the creative agent for that Mind.

In esoteric literature we are told that Lord Buddha is the "point of Light." He lives on the highest level of the Cosmic Physical Plane. The Divine Mind radiates Its Light throughout the world through this great Lord of Wisdom.

Stanza Two.

> *From the point of Love within the*
> *Heart of God*
> *Let love stream forth into the*
> *hearts of men.*
> *May Christ return to Earth.*

With this stanza, we invoke the second great energy, the energy of Love, the fountain of which is symbolically called the Heart of God. The Heart of God embraces the whole. In every manifested form there is a point of Love; there is a heart.

To give the simplest definition of love, we may say that it is the fire of life in man which awakens the consciousness of unity and inspires him to sacrifice everything to achieve consciousness of unity on larger scales and on higher levels of goodness and beauty.

In the progressive development of the human being, he first exists for himself. Gradually, he recognizes the existence of objects. Next, he becomes aware of the family, group, nation, and later, humanity as a whole.

Gradually, with enlightened consciousness, he penetrates the depths of existence and intuitively affirms that he is one cell in the body of the Great Existence — a cell which, in fact, is in communion with every other part of that Great Existence. When he realizes all of this, he tries to identify himself with and know himself as that Great Life.

The Invocation is directed first to the heart of every man, from which will pour out the love, the consciousness of unity — Love-Light. Such a person becomes a great beauty, a great healer, and a great liberator of human beings.

The center of Love found in the Heart of God is, first of all, the heart of man — because the heart of man is the only door through which one can reach the heart of humanity and gain access to the Heart of God. Also, the heart of man is the single fountainhead from which the Love of God can consciously pour Its liberating and transfiguring energy. The heart of man is a path which leads to that Great Heart, comprised of martyrs, saints, knowers, seers and resurrected ones of every nation.

It is the Love embodied in that center which is invoked in the second stanza of the *Great Invocation*, so that Christ may again appear on Earth to work out the blueprint which He anchored two thousand years ago. This time He will establish the Universal Kingdom of God on Earth.

To do this, the inherent Christ in every human heart should "descend on Earth," so that a new life on Earth starts — a life based on the consciousness of unity. This immanent Christ is not necessarily a religious man, or a devotee. He can be a living beauty in any social field — a strong leader radiating love; a man who is completely oriented to the happiness, success and liberation of mankind; a person who is in continuous contact with the Great Life Whom we call God, or Cosmic Consciousness, beyond the limitations of time and space.

That immanent Christ is the path through which the Universal Christ will reappear. As the sole leader and teacher, He will open a new way for humanity, leading to higher achievements and realizations of inner heights, inner Himalayas.

Unless we open the path within to the steps of the inner Christ, the "hope of Glory," we cannot feel the presence of that Great Existence Who, as the vision of perfection, a living beauty, has been leading humanity forward for two thousand years. According to His promise, He will appear again in the world.

May Christ return to Earth.

Who is Christ? He is the Leader of the Kingdom of God, the Leader of the Victorious Church. He is the embodiment of the divine principle of Love, the first one to reveal to mankind the true nature of God, and He has never left us. As He said, "Lo, I am with you all the days, even unto the end of the age."

May Christ return to Earth.

It is imperative to intensify the invocation for Love on a greater scale. Is there any other way to solve our problems — the problems in our homes, in our nations, in humanity?

All humanitarian aspirations, all plans for the betterment of human life in any field, are the answers to this ongoing invocation for Love and loving understanding. This will continue until Love dominates all our thoughts, feelings and actions, and demobilizes the forces of darkness, the forces of evil in the world. These are the forces which enslave the human heart, conscience and expression — by force, fear, money, glamor and illusion.

The Heart of God, the Love of God, nourishes the human conscience and consciousness like the sun. When obstacles found between Him and humanity are eliminated, when our hearts have become clean and more sensitive to higher impressions, we will have an unbroken relationship between Him and our hearts.

Christ is the stream of Love from God's Heart. At present, there are thousands in the world who feel His presence, His rays of Love, by which they are inspired, become transfigured, and sacrifice themselves for the welfare of humanity. Imagine the world which will come into existence as a result of this Invocation!

God is Love.

In one of the books dictated to Alice A. Bailey, Master Djwhal Khul says:

> . . . The basis of all Logoic action is love in activity, and the fundamental idea on which He bases action connected with the human Hierarchy is the power of love to drive onward, — call it evolution, if you like, call it inherent urge, should you so prefer, but it is love causing motion and urging onward to completion.[1]

---

[1] *A Treatise on White Magic*, p. 115.

Stanza Three.

> *From the centre where the*
> *Will of God is known*
> *Let purpose guide the little*
> *wills of men—*
> *The purpose which the Masters*
> *know and serve.*

Perhaps this is the most difficult verse to understand, though most world religions have prepared a way of approach. All religions symbolically tell us that God has His own Will, and that around His throne there are Entities of Fire Who are the immediate interpreters of His Will. These great Existences formulate His Will, and implement His Purpose. This Purpose stands as a magnetic center which draws to Itself all creation, each part according to its own capacity.

We are told that all true laws given to the world are a precipitation of that mighty center where the Will of God is known. These laws, as given in holy scriptures, direct human conduct in individual and group ways, toward the Central Magnet.

It is like a great symphony orchestra, in which the conductor is teaching a symphony to each instrumental section (the kingdoms of Nature), then trying to bring the whole together, gradually creating the ultimate rhythm and harmony which express the essential meaning of the symphony.

Each law, in any period, anywhere, is a way of translating the Central Will on a given level, through a given culture or civilization. It is mainly through legislation that governments are remote echoes of God's Will — if they are not distorted by their own separative interests. All true leaders receive their inspiration and courage from this center — mostly unconsciously — but in rare cases, consciously. This center propels the energy of Divine Will forward, so that in times of crisis, the energy of Divine Will becomes active within those who are dedicated to the welfare of humanity.

We are also told that in every human being there is a field of consciousness which is the vehicle of Divine Will. If we could penetrate into that level of consciousness, we could become impressed with Divine Will. This "vehicle" is sometimes called "the inner chamber," into which a person must enter and, after closing the "doors and windows," speak to God in intimate privacy.

From the human point of view, the "center where the Will of God is known" is the supreme focus of the highest aspirations and visions of all seers and martyrs — past, present and future. It is this center which must condition the activities of men on the physical, emotional and mental planes of man. Christ called this center, "My Father's House," where His Father's Will reigns.

The third stanza invokes the Will of God to, "[l]et purpose guide the little wills of men."

We have learned to say, "Thy Will be done, on Earth as it is in Heaven." We refer to the same center, the same fountain, the same energy when we try to align and harmonize our little wills with His Will.

Here we may say that the secret to everlasting peace and understanding among all nations rests in identifying human will with Divine Will. All our miseries, wars and sufferings are the result of friction between our own wills and God's Will.

Freedom is not a process of escaping from that Will. On the contrary, freedom is an act of approaching and identifying with that Will. The closer one approaches that Will, the more free he becomes. The farther he departs from that Will, the more misery and enslavement he experiences.

If we observe life on this planet, we see that humanity as a whole has evolved — a little here, a little there — physically, then on the emotional level, then on the mental level; first individually, then in group formation — then as a whole, on a universal scale.

With scientific advancement, people have observed how humanity and the Universe are conditioned by immutable Laws. These Laws are present not only on Cosmic levels, but also in solar, planetary, human, cellular and atomic fields. There is only One Law; all laws are subdivisions of that great Law.

All that exists is evolving, proceeding toward an unknown Purpose. The Central Magnet is drawing everything toward Itself. Is this not the reason why all cleavages eventually lead us to unity, all resistance to Light ultimately creates more light, all dictatorships increase an urge toward freedom, all hatred finally produces greater love and understanding? Being so, the True, the Beautiful and the Good are imminent, and are aspects of the Central Will.

Stanza Four.

> *From the centre which we call the*
> *race of men*
> *Let the Plan of Love and Light*
> *work out*
> *And may it seal the door where*
> *evil dwells.*

Here, the human race as a whole is taken as a center, a field of energy in which the Plan of Love and Light must work out. If we look at the human race as a whole, we see continuous upheaval in which contradictory forces, activities and directions meet, creating impassable chaos in all fields. This chaos can become a Cosmos only through Love and Light.

What is the Plan of Love and Light? One formula is, "Love your fellow man as yourself." Another is, "Search for the truth, and the truth will set you free." A large part of humanity has reached a stage where individuals dream and plan a creative life in the New Age. They dream of a good and beautiful life under the sun, free from hatred and ignorance.

The fourth stanza is a summary of age-long human aspiration, vision and hope. All three of these are directed toward Cosmic Consciousness as an invocation, so that the powers of Love and Light can "seal the door where evil dwells."

The word "evil" refers to any force which hinders the progress of humanity. The door of evil, from which such forces emerge to prevent the liberation and unity of humanity, is not only open in the hearts of individuals, but also in nations and in humanity as a whole.

The recognized evils at present are *materialism*, the spirit of *separation* and *totalitarianism*. Totalitarianism is our worst enemy in all areas of human life. We must seal the door to these three evils; in other words, their activity must be stopped.

Materialism, separatism and totalitarianism act as three evil forces in governments, in churches, in groups and nations. Most of the miseries of the world are the result of these three forces, because they foster injustice, fear and hatred — with the resultant tears and bloodshed.

If we perceive the misery of coming ages which will result from these three evil forces, then the invocation,

And may it seal the door where evil dwells

becomes the deepest call of the human heart.

Stanza Five.

> *Let Light and Love and Power restore*
> *the Plan on Earth.*

The final stanza of the *Great Invocation* synthesizes the entire Invocation and, like a great symphony, ascends toward the Central Heart. We are told that:

> The whole order of nature evinces a progressive march toward a higher life. There is a design in the action of the seemingly blindest forces. The whole process of evolution with its endless adaptations, is a proof of this.[2]

There is a Plan behind all creation. We cannot imagine laws without a plan, a plan without a purpose, nor a purpose without an originator — the "center where the Will of God is known." This is the department where higher intelligences study the Will of God, the Purpose of God.

The center we call the Love Center of God, is the Kingdom of God, having as its leader that great individual Whom we call the Christ. This is the department where the Purpose of God becomes the Plan for our planetary life. Humanity, the third center, will work out the Plan through its seven fields of endeavor: politics, religion, science, arts, philosophy, psychology and economics.

Every person has a high calling. The most sacred duty of a person is to find that high calling within himself, unveil it, and release it in its full expression in his daily life. The Ageless Wisdom suggests that the high calling of an individual is a portion of the Plan given to him, a strand of the overall Fabric — and the Plan is the high calling of all humanity. If one

---

[2]Blavatsky, Helena P., *The Secret Doctrine*, Vol. I, p. 298.

moves closer to his Soul, the Plan will gradually be unveiled. The Soul is part of the Plan.

It is not an easy task to establish the Kingdom of Love and Light within a person or a group. Humanity, through long ages of agony and suffering, is in a process of emerging from the dark night, moving toward the light and day of the Future.

This Invocation is a prayer for the Future, when humanity will bloom to its highest beauty and will express the music of the Purpose of the Infinite.

✳   ✳   ✳

As I enter my private room and sit on my chair to begin my daily meditation, I close my eyes and visualize millions of people who, with a single vision, stand in a boundless field and sound the *Great Invocation* with me.

I hear the voice of humanity, like a great ocean roar rising to the sky; and then, lightning suddenly flashes! The cloudy veil is pierced, unveiling the true Spiritual Sun. I see a path extending from humanity to the Spiritual Sun, and I see Christ climbing upward through each human heart, uplifting every man to his highest destiny.

> *Let Light and Love and Power restore*
> *the Plan on Earth.*

As you say the *Great Invocation*, visualize the whole world, all humanity, and spread Light, Love and Power all over the planet so that people everywhere, without distinction as to race, creed or color, are flooded:

- by the Light which cleanses away all ignorance and reveals the truth of the divine origin of man;

- by Love that urges us to live as one humanity, preparing the way for world brotherhood;
- by that Power which gives us the courage to live according to our highest vision, for the highest good of one humanity.

These visualizations are carried out during the pauses between stanzas, while saying the *Great Invocation*.

Through the process of meditation, you have expanded your consciousness, and perhaps you have even touched some higher planes, becoming charged with higher energies. Here, you can use that energy to broadcast your visions toward the whole world. This is a service which you can render to your fellow man, creating a magnetic vision for others, and a deep aspiration toward Light, Love and Power, so that they are able to "seal the door where evil dwells," to destroy and wipe away all crystallized thoughtforms of hatred, separation and evil created over the centuries.

The *Great Invocation* is a potent healing mantram. It clears away all obstacles in the three worlds of the personality, letting divine energy flow throughout the human vehicles, carrying fires that heal, unify and transform through all human and planetary forms.

The *Great Invocation* builds bridges or communication lines between the etheric heart, throat and head centers. The radiations of these centers interpenetrate one another, creating an electric shield of protection around the personality. The influence of the mantram then expands and touches the point of Power, the point of Love, and the point of Light in the Universe. These energies, flowing into you and through you, are then directed to the whole Universe, especially to those places which need cleaning and healing — places of bloodshed; places where human dignity is debased; places where the energies of the human body, emotions and mind are being wasted; places which hinder the circulatory life energy, creating stagnant "lakes" and infected areas on the planetary body. Like a great beam of light, the energy of the *Great Invocation* must be directed into these dark places.

We must mention that such degenerated places may receive excessive energy and become even more stimulated in their direction of activity. Corruption, bloodshed and crime may increase, but if the current of energy steadily pours down upon such places, Light will gradually increase and existing vices will begin to disintegrate. In this way, many illusions and glamors are destroyed, prison bars are removed, and prisoners are set free.

In doing such sacred work, we must be very careful not to project our own glamors and illusions toward objects, and not to build any specific thoughtforms about individuals, groups, nations or events. Instead, we must stand in the light of the Soul, and release the energy in a general, objective way, toward physical, emotional and mental locations, leaving the energy free to carry out the work of burning, cleaning and clearing away obstacles on the path of progress. By being a clear channel for these energies, events will occur in tune with the Divine Plan, and in accordance with the karma of the point of focus.

To clarify this point, let us say that if we direct energy toward an individual who is ill, or who is in glamor or illusion, we visualize the individual and send him the triple energies of Light, Love and Power, so as to form an atmosphere of these three energies around him. We may visualize a nightclub or a war zone, and pour these energies there. In all the forgoing examples, we must send Light, Love and Power without demanding any specific effect, without imagining the way we want the sick person to be, or trying to change the point of focus of any individual or group. We must only create the proper conditions, and then let things happen as they should, according to the karma involved.

If the person to whom we direct the energies passes away or acts in a way toward us that we did not expect, we must maintain our indifference, knowing that good happens in a way that is often beyond our comprehension or calculations.

In other words, we must not determine the outcome. Our duty is to steadily shed Light, Love and Power, without identifying ourselves with persons, locations or events, cultivating a high level of indifference toward the results.

By sounding the *Great Invocation* in this way, we use our visualization, concentration and will power, which will effectively transport the energy to the intended location and set it loose there.

Will power is not used to force, rule or change anything the way we want it; it is used to carry the triple energies of Light, Love and Power to Their destination.

First, you will spread this triple energy all over the planet; in cases of emergency, you can project it toward specific individuals, groups, parties, nations and locations. Thus, you will learn to direct Divine Energy, and become a white magician. But remember: a white magician is a person who stands in the light of his Soul, and operates from that vantage point with the soul aspect of all forms.

11

Cooperation Between Groups

*T*he *Great Invocation*, which is the core of all triangles, is not limited to any race, religion, doctrine, philosophy or political belief. Any group which is dedicated to the service of humanity can use this Invocation, and thus create a point of understanding, cooperation and fusion with all those who are using the same Invocation.

Such cooperation in triangle work for light, goodwill and will-to-good will eventually create a great field of energy which will serve as an agent of distribution for the energy of the Hierarchy and Shamballa to humanity.

Through triangles, all people of goodwill will relate to each other; all those who have great aspiration to serve humanity will draw energy from each other. All those who actively work to salvage the world will know each other. Through these relationships, a mass network of cooperation will be established across this planet.

Some people with a mystical inclination believe that the world is filled with evil people; this is not true. There are many more good people than harmful people; the problem is that the people of goodwill are not in contact with each other. They are not organized into a nation or located in a common place to make their will respected and their voices heard. They are scattered throughout all nations. But triangle work will solve this problem. People will cultivate such respect, love and gratitude for each other that they will find the ways and means to work together on a project centered around a great vision for all humanity. Once the people of goodwill are organized, world affairs will radically change.

All organized activities eventually fail if there is not a continuous supply of Love, Light and Power. Triangles steadily channel and are a source of the Light, Love and Energy of the Hierarchy. As a collective group, triangles will even be impressed by Shamballa energy. Charged with such a voltage, the men and women of Light, Love and Power will move mountains and pave the way for a greater culture, for a greater civilization.

It is imperative that various unrelated groups use this mantram as the world mantram. There is nothing in this mantram that damages the integrity of any group, decreases its influence upon its members, or diminishes its income.

Those groups which are oriented toward active goodwill, motivated by a love for humanity, can use this mantram without the slightest change. This mantram, in its final analysis, is a formula for energy, a great symbol which carries incredible power. Any group can translate its own highest intentions through such a symbol and receive energy by applying its formula.

Some Definitions.

To present a more complete concept regarding the key words found in the mantram, we can say:

God: the living whole; the consciousness behind all creation.

Light: the power of revelation.

Love: the energy of attraction and cooperation.

Purpose: the Good toward which all creation is oriented.

Masters: those great Beings Who, after having graduated from human evolution, now act as points of inspiration for all mankind.

Christ: the ideal of all human efforts; the symbol of true love and sacrificial service; the spearhead of human striving.

The Plan: the explanation of the laws of Nature and of the purpose of the cycle. Being so, it is the surest path to follow to develop and unfold ourselves. It is the easiest way to end the suffering of humanity, and a guarantee for ever-expanding joy and achievement for human efforts.

The Will of God: the highest good for all existence.

Evil: that which creates hindrances to unfoldment; that which distracts us from the path of Light and Love; that which weakens our striving toward perfection.

The *Great Invocation* is so inclusive that no one who desires to serve humanity and loves humanity in his heart can reject it.

When I was in the Middle East, serving as the principal of a secondary school, there were many political currents in the school because of parental involvement and influence, and because of the influence of certain political parties. After studying the situation, I presented the *Great Invocation* as an opening invocation at faculty meetings. At first there was no apparent reaction. After a while, some of the teachers began using it before starting their classes. A little later, the entire student body gathered in a big hall every morning and repeated it together. In a few months, it had spread into the families related to the school. Eventually it built a great spirit of cooperation, which helped us accomplish many positive changes in the school, buy new property, and build better facilities for the students.

This Invocation does not harm any group, any interest. Any group can use the Invocation as its own. In a short time, its power will manifest as the spirit of cooperation, of construction, understanding and striving toward greater achievement.

The *Great Invocation* must not only be recited. Musicians must create notes and music for it, so that it can be sung by the multitudes. Great painters and artists must demonstrate the *Great Invocation* through color and symbol, revealing greater depth and understanding to us. Writers must try to explain its various phrases, and express its beauty through poems, lyrics and prose. It must even be presented in the form of symbolic dancing and movement, in rituals and ceremonies.

Advanced psychologists must observe its effect on the human psyche, and reveal other aspects of the *Great Invocation*. Doctors can cooperate with these other professionals by observing the healing effects that the Invocation has on their patients. Higher clairvoyants and those with psychic gifts must observe the subjective effects of the Invocation upon etheric centers, the aura, and the network of world energies. It must be scientifically tested and researched to reveal its vibratory effect, voltage, frequency and radioactivity, and its possible effect on human liberation. Politicians can engage themselves in observing the social effects of such an organized, invocative and evocative activity.

Through these united observations, demonstrations and results, we will have greater hope — a greater future for all humanity. Actually, all that the *Great Invocation* does is to relate humanity to its own vision, to the Hierarchy, and to make it sensitive to the Will of the Almighty One.

*I*ndex

Works by Torkom Saraydarian:

Bhagavad Gita
Challenge for Discipleship
Christ, The Avatar of Sacrificial Love
Cosmic Shocks
Cosmos in Man
A Daily Discipline of Worship
Dialogue with Christ
Fiery Carriage and Drugs
Five Great Mantrams of the New Age
Flame of Beauty, Culture, Love, Joy
Hiawatha and the Great Peace
Hidden Glory of the Inner Man
Hierarchy and the Plan
Irritation—The Destructive Fire
I Was
Joy and Healing
Legend of Shamballa
Psyche and Psychism
Questioning Traveler and Karma
Science of Becoming Oneself
Science of Meditation
Sex, Family and the Woman in Society
Spring of Prosperity
Symphony of the Zodiac
Synthesis
Talks on Agni
Torchbearers
Triangles of Fire
Unusual Court
Woman, Torch of the Future

CALL OR FAX TO ORDER:
SARAYDARIAN INSTITUTE
P. O. Box 267 · Sedona · AZ 86339
Phone 520-282-2655 ◆ Fax 520-282-0514